Loan Officer Champions

Case Studies from Top Producers

Carl White

MORTGAGE MARKETING ANIMALS

Published by
Mortgage Marketing Animals

Copyright ©2022 The Marketing Animals
Printed in the United States of America

ISBN: 978-1-7324655-5-8

MORTGAGE MARKETING ANIMALS
Palm Harbor, FL
MortgageMarketingAnimals.com

Dedication

This book is a series of interviews of Loan Officer Champions that were done and then put in book form. I'm truly honored to know each of these amazing people and to have played a role in helping them achieve extraordinary success. Now they are inspiring tens of thousands of loan officers across the country.

But none of this would have ever happened if not for two of the most wonderful ladies who helped me create a wildly successful mortgage business, then a loan officer training company that has literally changed countless lives. They both believed in me before I even believed in myself. I'm forever grateful for their wisdom, knowledge, direction, hard work and, most of all, for their love and friendship.

So Diane Ranger and Tammy Schneider, it is a true privilege to dedicate this book to you.

Foreword

I met Carl White about fourteen years ago. We were both emerging out of the mortgage crisis of 2008–2009 as industry leaders and influencers. Over the years, we've worked in parallel in different capacities within the industry. Carl went on to build the best coaching program the mortgage industry has ever seen, and I went on to become the co-creator and co-host of *The National Real Estate Post*, gaining nationwide recognition as an industry leader. Through the course of time, working together or side-by-side in various ways, we've become very close friends. The thing I admire most about Carl is his overwhelming kindness and generosity. Carl is always "at the ready" to help. He's consistently complimentary, kind, light-hearted, and ready to bestow upon whomever he's engaging with his experience, knowledge, and advice.

If you ever have the opportunity to be the beneficiary of his experience, knowledge, and advice, drink it up, take notes, and hang on to it because it's probably exactly what you need to hear. As for anyone who might wonder if Carl truly has the right stuff when it comes to helping a loan officer go from say two loans a month to 100 loans a month, consider this; many people don't realize that Carl runs a mortgage team that closed over $1.2 Billion in business last year. And let's not forget his purchase-to-refi ratio was 72% purchase, 28% refinance, and he did it all based on the methods, procedures, and hiring practices he teaches his coaching students. So, uh, yeah.

Speaking of his coaching students, let's talk about this book. I love this book because it's not written by Carl—it's written by his students. What a brilliant idea! Instead of "bragging about what he can do for you", he simply lets a handful of his students tell their story on how they got into the business and how, at some point, they made the "pivot" from average to stardom.

The loan officers in this book who shared their stories are all unique individuals with unique circumstances, but there is a common thread they all share. That common thread is that, when they reached a point in their career where they couldn't figure out how to go any further, they took the plunge to join the Freedom Club Coaching Program. It was at that point they each learned how to "work on" their business instead of "working in" their business. They went from having time-sucking mentally-exhausting jobs to running fine-tuned high-volume/high-revenue businesses, all while freeing up their personal time, affording them the ability to spend more time on the things that are most important to them.

The backstory behind all the loan officers in this book is what I found most intriguing. Sometimes when we see the numbers of the most successful loan officers in the country, we may feel like there was something special going on with them...some kind of advantage that average loan officers don't have. It's simply not the case.

Some of the loan officers in this book are on that list of top loan officers in the country and, when you hear their stories, you'll be pleasantly surprised to find out they were just like any other average loan officer. The only difference is that one day they decided to get the proper coaching/training/education needed to learn how to run their businesses correctly. They found out how to do only the things that they're good at, that they like to do, and that generate the most income. They've built skilled teams to do all the other stuff. This is what the Freedom Club teaches you. This is how you go from working a time-sucking job to running a successful business. Don't take it from me or Carl—take it from the successful loan officers and branch managers who contributed to this book.

Dive into this book. Read the stories. See what these successful loan officers would tell themselves if they could go back ten years. Their advice will save you a lot of time and heartache. I'm excited for you. I'm excited because I know when you read these stories that you'll find YOU. You are in one of these stories—right now!

Look, it doesn't matter what level of business you're doing, there's always another level. The cool thing is that this "new level" can be achieved—took candid interviews, stories, and real-world experiences from top loan officers and compiled them here.

It was important for me to gather what you're about to read for several reasons: inspiration, education, seeing the clues success leaves behind...and to acknowledge just how far these loan officer champions have come to succeed against the odds that presented in life and business.

—Frank Garay
Co-Creator of The National Real Estate Post
Mortgage Industry Leader and Influencer

Contents

Introduction

Given what I do in supporting mortgage loan officers around the country to work less while making more in their businesses, I get to have valuable time with very successful loan officers. Over the years, I have learned so much from these conversations; in fact, I've often thought I should have recorded them to share with others. That's exactly what I did in this book—I took candid interviews, stories, and real-world experiences from top loan officers and compiled them here.

It was important for me to gather what you're about to read for several reasons: inspiration, education, seeing the clues success leaves behind...and to acknowledge just how far these loan officer champions have come to succeed against the odds that presented in life and business.

These loan officer champions were personally selected by me because they are everyday folks who figured out that the number of work hours is independent of income. They 'got' that it's about humility, putting family first, and being a good person to be good at business.

Just a few of the key insights you'll read include:

- Challenges ARE the path.
- Resilience builds strength.
- There are opportunities in chaos.

- It's vital to get comfortable with being uncomfortable.
- You can have a good life AND an epic mortgage loan business.

After reading these case studies, I am sure you will be inspired and I want to hear about that. Please share your thoughts on the FB wall here and/or drop me a line at **Facebook.com/ LoanOfficer-BreakfastClub**.

Frankly, I want to help you become successful too so I'll be sharing how you can get started for free. As you'll soon see, taking just one right action can change everything for you and your business.

I hope you enjoy these champions and their stories as much as I did putting them together.

The Accidental Loan Officer

By Tammy Saul
Owner and President
Federal Hill Mortgage Company

I became a loan officer by accident. It happened at a time when I thought my professional life was over.

In 2003, I was a practicing attorney with a master's degree in business. While I was working, I met and started dating a guy who was a mortgage loan officer and director of sales at a mortgage company. My employer, a big law firm, required new associates to meet production quotas for billable hours. For two consecutive years, I didn't meet those quotas and so I was fired. I was in my mid-20's so this was a devastating blow to my career (or so I thought at the time).

It was mentally and emotionally one of my lowest points; I thought my life was over. Here I was, after investing tens of thousands of dollars into law and business school, after going through hell to pass the law exam, and after entering a highly competitive job market post 9/11, rejected for lack of performance and without a job. My boyfriend (now my husband) seemed to enjoy his job so I decided to join him for just a few months as I applied for new positions in the legal field. My thought process was nothing more than 'let me try this mortgage thing out for a little bit.' That decision changed the course of my life.

From day one, I had zero intention of "doing mortgages" long-term. The dilemma? I did very well very quickly, out producing every seasoned loan officer in my branch within my first three months. I did things my way rather than how the mortgage company owner taught, which meant my new job couldn't last forever. In 2005, after less than 18 months of experience and with no formal training in sales, my new husband and I decided to open our own mortgage company.

That decision was easier said than done. The challenges were, and are, plentiful, and they continue to change over time. If I had to pick just one significant and most likely common challenge for small business owners and people in my industry, it is to acquire and retain quality talent.

Great Talent Requires Personal Development

Great talent is not just about finding good people and then hiring them. That's the superficial piece. Instead, it's about developing yourself as a business owner and leader to attract the right talent who will want to come work for and with you. Ironically, acquiring the right talent is about dealing with your own personal issues that arise through the course of building your business. I frequently went through intense self-development and profound personal growth to be able to appreciate certain personalities and cultivate the ability to work with all kinds of different people.

Personally, I struggled with this lesson, especially in the beginning, because I was so intense. I went to business school. I went to law school. I was extremely driven but I was also critical to a fault, a quality that deterred others. In the beginning, I only had one employee. I had to become that person who other people wanted to work for, which took an unforeseen and sometimes daunting level of personal growth and self-discovery. Amazingly, that first team member is still with me today; in fact, she is the boss here now, managing and directing everyone else. I credit that to her being an extraordinary individual who consistently overlooked my personality flaws over the years. Most people aren't like that because it takes an uncommon generosity of spirit and sustained commitment over time.

Today, I have a company that has grown consistently year over year; just last week, we hired our 12th employee. We will close over $200 million in loans this year—and that's with me originating 99% of the company's business. It is amazing what's possible when you build from a foundation of investing in self-growth and constant self-correction.

Another challenge worth mentioning is that I had to learn who NOT to work with in my business. Many of the people who took my time—especially in the beginning—did not enrich me or my business. I worked with them because I thought I had to and from a mindset of scarcity. In fact, they caused me (and therefore my family) great stress, putting pressure on my business to a magnitude I didn't realize until they walked away or I eliminated them. They did not enrich the company and held us back from reaching that next level.

Once I learned how to let go of what wasn't working for me, I attracted better quality relationships. Now when I perceive a toxic relationship, I more easily release that connection. I'm okay with saying, "I'm not the right one for you." I have confidence in knowing that release will create space for the right person to come into my business, which is predictably what happens every time.

Let Go of Toxicity and Build Faster

If I could go back in time and tell myself what to have done differently sooner, I would tell myself this:

1) Let toxic relationships and people go. Tolerating them does not make you a hero. I held on to some for years. I remember my state

of mind then: It was one of fear of loss, scarcity. I feared emptiness, having nothing. The scarcity mentality drove my decision-making. I didn't appreciate my gift for attracting people and business. Toxic relationships cloud your vision but you must let them go. When you do, your life will change. I had to clear the fog and be willing to risk loss in order to gain better business relationships. One of my favorite sayings is "feel the fear and then do it anyway." Once you can discipline yourself to not fear scarcity, you will live in a mindset of purposeful abundance and, thereby, attract abundance.

That scarcity pattern can run deep. Even today, I still question my judgment and certain relationships. Almost always, my intuition is right in the end about what and who positively fuels me and my business. Earlier this year, I had a top-producing agent about whom my staff consistently complained; they told me repeatedly she was abrasive, hostile and a micromanager; yet, I continued working with her. I allowed it to go longer than it should have before letting her go. My point is that even fifteen years into my mortgage career, and knowing what I know now, I still hesitated. That old scarcity-based thinking kicked in—after all, she brought a lot of business and I feared losing it. What inevitably happened was, once I let that fear and the relationship go, my business improved. Letting go of toxic relationships has always, every single time, opened the door to something better. Most of the time, you don't know what that "better" thing or person is or what it will look like. Or you think you know what it will look like but then it ends up being something completely different.

When you employ people, your responsibility is to discern the good stress from the type of stress that brings you down. When a relationship brings you down, it creates a ripple effect to everyone in the company, putting at risk the livelihood of the wonderful people you've invested time and resources attracting, recruiting, training, and working with . . . that's a big price tag to pay for any amount of business. It might be a difficult decision—until you remember why you're doing it. You are protecting your greatest assets—you and your team—and opening the space for the right relationships to show up and want to work with you. It's the law of attraction in action!

2) The other insight I would give my then-self is to build a team faster. For years, I hesitated to hire people. Part of it was because I didn't feel I had the predictable production to hire (and pay for) employees. Part of it was my own growth process to become that someone for whom people wanted to work. I was difficult, intense, demanding and picky. And I'm still all those things! The difference is now I'm much more human, and people want to work for human people. I had to learn to delegate and trust my team in creating results, have compassion in understanding why things weren't always done as I expected, and learn how to create a supportive work environment. In turn, my employees gave me back that support to help me grow further.

My company is now at a place where the people who work with me really love being here. They appreciate the leadership and the vision. They're enrolled in the vision, and they've been a part of seeing it come to life. Again, that all started with me working on myself over years.

Become an Expert

When a loan officer wants to take their business to the next level, whether they're closing a few loans a month or thirty, if they're new to the industry, they must first become a subject matter expert. They have to become masters of their craft and experts in providing value to their customers. That craft is knowledge and the ability to effectively apply that vast knowledge to guide and advise others to want to take action to better themselves. It comes from listening more than talking. It comes from guiding vs. commanding or selling.

Loan officers need to take themselves out of the 'I'm a salesperson and have to sell this mortgage' mentality to become an expert in what they do so they can provide a better experience and greater value to their clients. I was successful "doing mortgages" from the beginning largely because this was already my mode of thinking as an attorney. Attorneys are not salespeople—they are problem-solvers and advisors. Attorneys think outside the box and produce creative and frequently many layered solutions to benefit their clients. They then support through the end of that process in an advisory role. That is how I have approached every mortgage loan client from day one, and it is opposite to the way I was taught when I first ventured into the industry in 2003.

On my first day as a loan officer, I was put into a chair and given a computer, a phone and a script to call dialer leads. Imagine the culture shock, coming from the practice of law where there was some dignity. There was honor in being an attorney. I had a plaque on my door with my name on it, my degree meant something, and business was done with some decorum. However, as a new loan officer in the 2003 subprime boom, I was instantly pushed to the bottom of the barrel. It was the opposite end of my accustomed professional spectrum. I was given a list of dialer leads to call, handed a script, and told to, "call these people and don't deviate from this script" I was terrified and disgusted at the same time. However, even more than that, I was determined to make the most of what I intended to be merely a short-lived mortgage gig until I found my next legal job.

Nonetheless, for the first few calls, I did exactly what I was told because I'm coachable. As I got further into it, I trashed the script and decided to do this MY way—the way I was taught to professionally handle clients in business and law school. I became the advisor. I'm glad the company owner didn't hear me in the beginning because he would have called me out on the spot. Instead of using canned words, I just talked with people, giving them advice and direction based on what I knew.

At that point, I wasn't a subject matter expert—but I figured it out very quickly. Every loan officer needs to do the same—take yourself up a notch by becoming a subject matter expert and mortgage loan advisor. Yes, we're in this profession to make money and run a business. But it's a different mentality to go sell mortgages vs. advise clients on their mortgage needs and process. Not only will the latter approach bring you more business, but it's also much more gratifying personally. People can sniff out a salesperson from a mile away—nobody likes that. People don't want to be sold; they want to be guided and directed, especially when they're a first time homebuyer. Coincidentally, employees don't want to work for a salesperson; instead, they want leadership and professionalism. Once you become that professional to your clients (notice I call them clients not customers), your team will follow suit, respect you, and rally around the established culture.

Additionally, you'll never need to buy leads either—I never have and never will. In fact, I don't like the word "lead." My office doesn't use the word "lead" or "customer." We say "referrals" or "clients." Experts and professionals build relationships that organically attract referrals. Cultivate relationships from those you already know for a successful business. Exhaust your warm market first. Call me boring but this is the traditional business model that never fails: be an expert. Take care of people, be virtuous, be honest and work hard. People will notice and they will not only come back to you for their second, third, and fourth mortgage but they will also send their friends and family, who will—in turn—send their friends and family. Organic and natural growth occurs from doing the right thing consistently over time.

To this day, I still haven't exhausted my warm market. This month will be my best month yet after being in business for fifteen years, closing somewhere between 80–100 loans. After these 80–100 loans close, I'll have over 150 in my pipeline still and we are projecting to close $200–$210 million in volume in just this year. Again, I don't buy leads. I don't pay for marketing. I simply speak to my warm market and develop new relationships. My team and I do an excellent job for people. We treat people well. We ask for business from the business we already have, which is consistent with Carl White's teachings. Carl White and Tammy Schneider are my coaches; this is what they teach and what I've been following for years. The moment I started following their advice is the moment my business exploded exponentially.

Just this month, CNBC chose me, my company, and my team to be on their new show 'Financing the American Dream.' The invitation came at my busiest hour in business but it was an opportunity I couldn't refuse. The show will feature the nation's top producers to showcase our industry. When their production team arrives here, I'll show them the city, interview a few agents, and then take them through our office. It's a wonderful opportunity to connect with my agents and show off my city.

Feel the Fire

What works for me today is not what worked for me when I was new. This most recent month in business has been my best production-wise; however, the actual work of advising and structuring loans is now easy. I do what I do so unconsciously that it's hard to break down that strategy for others. Who I am and how I work are intertwined. And, of course, now I have a team to help me.

The baseline is just hard work. From an early age, I've always worked hard and had that proverbial fire in my belly to succeed. As a first-generation immigrant brought up with the American Dream ideal, I grew up with a profound gratitude for being in a country of such great potential. When I see opportunity, I can't help but go for it. That's just an integral part of my personality reinforced by my upbringing. Being on the "Financing the American Dream" show is, in that regard, a full-circle experience. When looking to add another individual to my team, I look for that "fire" in their belly. It can't be taught—you either have it or you don't.

So naturally, when I was thrown into the mortgage industry with so much opportunity to make a tremendous amount of money, my head spun with possibilities. I thought, 'why wouldn't I want to work night and day to make it in this business because there's so much it offers?' The business is a particularly lucrative one when you already work hard with great efficiency; these characteristics were already inherent to my core.

I also had a competitive advantage over the typical 2003 loan officer because I was educated. Clients frequently remarked that I was "unlike other loan officers." Other loan officers were trained in sales; I was trained in how to be a professional. Most of the time, I didn't share that background with prospective clients; I just advised them and let them discern the benefit and difference on their own. Now it's clear from my signature and website but back then (pre-website-era), I didn't even bring it up unless someone asked or questioned why my advice was so different from the "other loan officers."

When speaking with someone, I would not only give advice but also other outside-the-box insight or wisdom that addressed their needs. Frequently, it was unrelated to the direct matter at hand. People felt and responded to that personal touch. They learned from what I shared and knew they could rely on me to tell them without any fluff. And that was how I built my business in the beginning. I created magical experiences for others. They felt that in my perspective, expertise, and dedication to holistically supporting them in getting the right mortgage. As a result, they talked about me to other people they knew. I then recreated that level of insightful experience for those other people and for the others they referred, who in turn referred others, who in turn referred others. I didn't really have to work at building connections; I just focused on genuinely caring enough to give them practical expertise they could use.

When I was brand-new in the business, I met a real estate agent. Well, actually he wasn't a real estate agent at the time; back then, he was a real estate investor buying a piece of property. I met him and was just so excited to have a new client that I went over the top to impress him. I was responsive to him day and night. He called whenever he needed anything and I did everything for him. He was tough on me, but my determination and persistence won him over.

Fast-forward fifteen years and that one individual—who became an agent ten years after we met—has since referred hundreds of people to me. He's introduced me to other real estate agents who have introduced me to other real estate agents who have introduced me to other clients.

I've mentioned I should have let some relationships go sooner than later. At the same time, I also developed relationships with some really great people who led me to other great people. I just had to continue being amazing in delivering value and showing up for each person who came my way. That's a core piece of my personal growth and development—growing through client relationships as well as with my team.

Business is a lot easier now because I have relationships that have been cultivated over time, often for many years. Whether we have known each other for a long time or are new to each other, I continue to deliver amazing knowledge and service for my clients and real estate agent partners both to honor our connection and to be top of mind for their referrals. That's why it is so important to discern my best relationships; there is only so much time and energy available for that level of premium service.

One of the biggest differences now is I have a team. I invest a great deal of my time teaching them how to conduct business in a way that retains clients and brings us more business. For example, a great deal of the business I'm closing currently consists of past clients, referrals from past clients or real estate agents I've known for a while. They're not people I met through cold-calling—I don't solicit phone calls or leads, nor do I buy Zillow leads. I could but I choose not to because, again, warm markets are always the best markets.

Altogether, my main strategies for closing more deals has expanded over time from the seeds I planted when new in the industry: be a subject matter expert and trusted advisor, deliver high-value service, attract and retain people who appreciate and support what I do, invest in my team, work my relationships as warm markets, and keep growing myself as a leader and business owner.

Monumental Shift through Coaching

When I hired Carl White and Tammy Schneider as my coaches a year and a half ago, my business shifted in a tremendous way. Tremendous isn't a good word—it's nowhere sufficient in describing the powerhouse results. Monumental is a better word to describe the shift that my business experienced—and fast.

I listened to Carl White's podcast, **LoanOfficerFreedom.com**, for two years before I even approached him for personalized coaching. I remember it was when I started listening to those podcasts that I started hearing things I've always thought I should do but didn't because I thought they were crazy and nobody else was doing them. Then I would hear Carl talk about them. My instincts were validated and, as I applied what I heard and felt was right for my clients, referral partners and team, my business exploded.

In 2016, I closed $54 million in business, in 2017, $67 million, in 2018, $72 million and, in 2019, the year that Carl and Tammy accepted me as their student, I closed $140 million. That means I doubled my business from the prior year. My daughter was also born that year through a high-risk pregnancy at the age of 43. This year I will close over $200 million in loans, about a 50% increase over the previous year. That outcome is 100% the result of the coaching I received and applied in my business. You can't just hire a coach and expect results. You can't just learn what to do and not follow through on it. You have to do the work.

There were many things they told me to do that I didn't want to do . . . things that were uncomfortable to act on and which scared the heck out of me. But everything they told me to do was always right. Their guidance was always on target. From the time my business started benefitting from their advice, I stopped questioning them. The most exciting piece for me isn't really even what I've done so far but what next year looks like because of the team I've built, thanks to my amazing coaches. I have never had my systems in place the way I have them in place right now. I've never had the benefit of this tight of an organization with so much support.

In fact, this coming year could be a $300 million loan production year. We could potentially close a hundred loans every month. When you close a hundred loans in one month, you see how it works and how it can happen. In your mind, by doing it once you create for yourself a new baseline and a new standard. You can close a hundred loans a month every single month because you've done it. So that's what I see 2021 bringing my company—consistently closing 100 loans per month.

Going for #1

With Carl White's and Tammy Schneider's transformational business coaching, my business will unquestionably continue to grow, and exponentially. One of their many lessons is that Freedom isn't instant; nor is it free initially. There is a cost and a personal growth investment. Once those dues are paid, however, the payoff is enormous and fast-moving.

For years, I was a trapped loan officer closing 6–10 loans a month with little quality of life. Now I'm closing 80–100 a month with a 4-year old and 16-month old at home. While I still work hard, I no longer work "crazy." Most importantly, I limit my activities to those I enjoy or that are essential, and I'm working with realtors, clients, and employees who fulfill me rather than those I would have chosen previously from a scarcity mindset.

If I continue upon this current trajectory, I don't think I can even fathom the possibilities. I know I'll make it to the #1 loan officer spot in my state by next year (Currently #2). After that? The sky's the limit.

Could I get to be the number one loan officer in the country? It's possible! I know exactly who holds that spot now . . . I know what he's doing and I'm watching him. In 2019, he closed over $600 million in loans. If I can close $300 million loans in 2021, assuming I continue developing business, growing my team, following my coaches, and making the right decisions, then why wouldn't my business increase by 50% or even 100% year over year? Not only is it possible, but it's already happening now.

Live the American Dream

I was born in the former Soviet Union. In 1979, my parents (in their twenties, still just kids themselves) made the bold decision to escape their homeland to give me (then three) and my brother (then two) a better life here. Their courage is the platform on which my company stands today.

We grew up poor, not having much more than an appreciation of the American Dream. Every day, my parents would remind us,

"Do you know how lucky you are to be here? Do you know what you have here?" As a kid, I would roll my eyes at hearing this over and over. But over time, it inspired and stoked that fire in my belly, that relentless and compelling drive to make the most of every good opportunity presented to me. Some people think I'm crazy but I can't help the way I am; it is also the reason my company is what it is today—successful and growing.

Several years after we left the Soviet Union, Chernobyl, which was just a short distance from where I lived, experienced a horrific nuclear accident. Many people died. Children were born deformed. People lost their vision, their hearing, and their sight. And the corrupt government in power hid the explosion from the people so they continued to drink the water and breathe contaminated air without filters. It was just terrible.

Had my parents not risked everything to bring me out of the Soviet Union at that young age, I would still be there, poor, uneducated and living in meager conditions. I may never have had children.

I grew up with the vision of the American Dream. The American Dream is really cultural, an ideal woven through the fabric of daily life and business. The American Dream is what makes our company what it is . . . and every U.S.-based loan officer has the opportunity to reach up and grab a piece of that dream for themselves. Don't wait. Do it starting now. You don't know what the future can bring you unless you create it for yourself.

About Tammy Saul

Meet Tammy Saul, JD, MBA

Tammy Saul, founding member of Federal Hill Mortgage in 2006, is an award-winning loan originator who has been recognized as a top producer nationally since 2016. In 2019 and 2020, Tammy was ranked #1 in Baltimore, #2 in Maryland and #80 nationwide across several hundred thousand loan originators. As of November 2020, she is officially in the top 35 Female Mortgage Loan Officers nationwide (and #1 female mortgage originator in Maryland) per the official Scotsman Guide rankings.

In her busiest month in business, Tammy was selected to host and represent Maryland and D.C. for CNBC's *Financing The American Dream*, which will air monthly through December 2021. Tammy is one of the most sought-after loan officers in the industry; in November 2020, she closed 85+ loans totaling over $30 million in loan volume, making 2020 a $200 million+ production year.

Tammy earned her MBA from the University of Baltimore in 1999 and her Juris Doctor (J.D.) from the University of Maryland in 2001. To this day, Tammy continues to hold her license to practice law but chooses to do what fulfills her most: making the American Dream of homeownership possible through sound, honest, reliable, and professional mortgage planning of the highest caliber.

Tammy can be reached at:

Email: **tammyl@federalhillmortgage.com**

Phone: 800-551-9198

Website: **federalhillmortgage.com/**

Facebook: **facebook.com/FederalHillMortgageMD/**

LinkedIn: **linkedin.com/company/federal-hill-mortgage/**

Trust Yourself and Your People

By Jennifer Conley
Vice President of Branch Operations
Hometown Lenders

Like a lot of people in this business, I became a loan officer by chance. Way back when, I had a government job. I don't know why I ever thought I could be a government worker, but I tried it for a short time and, not surprisingly, it did not work out. I ended up taking the summer off.

When it was time to go back to work, I couldn't find anything. I ended up at an insurance sales job. I had also done a phone interview with a mortgage company but I took the insurance job instead. At the insurance job, I had to travel and be away from my kids, who were small at the time. After I was gone for two days, I thought, 'I can't do this.'

As I was driving home that second day, I drove past the aforementioned mortgage company. They had called me for a second interview. I took it as a sign that I drove right past their office that day, and I called them when I got home. They said, "Sure, come in on Friday."

I was hired for the position, which involved selling leads to mortgage companies, and after a couple of months, they noticed I was the only one who sold anything. The management team approached me and said, "Hey, why don't you go over to the mortgage side? You'll make more money because you're a good salesperson. We think you would be a better fit there." And so, by happenstance and because I wanted to be with my kids, I became a loan officer.

Initially, my biggest challenge in this business was learning how to make the phone ring. When I first got started, we were given leads purchased by the company, and the phone just rang. However, after 2008, the phone stopped ringing because it wasn't a great way to get business anymore.

It was hard to get refinances done, so we had to learn how to close business without refis. I had to up my game by learning how to work with realtors, getting them to trust me, and asking them to send me their clients. That pivot point helped us to grow the business, but it was probably the biggest challenge I had in the beginning.

Let Other People Help You

As time went on, the challenges changed. I'm a recovering control freak, so it was a test for me to learn to give up control and allow people to help me. One of my biggest personal challenges was learning I'm not always right and that there are people who know how to do it differently, and maybe even better. That was a hard lesson to learn; however, it has been extremely valuable.

I overcame those challenges by immersing myself in research. When I want to do something, I try to learn it by osmosis—I just jump into it one hundred percent. In doing that, I met Carl White. I'd gone to one of his events and I watched him over several years. I joined the Mortgage Marketing Animals (MMA), and eventually, they started a coaching group. I thought, 'Oh, I'm going to try this.' I figured if their "free" stuff and their starter program had gotten me this far, imagine what one-on-one coaching would do.

I knew coaching with Carl was going to be a big investment, yet something inside me knew I needed to do it. It was a really big check to write, and I didn't have the money at the time, but I did it anyway. I was scared. I didn't know how I would make those payments every month. In the end, it was the best check I ever wrote.

As time went on, Carl and his partner Tammy taught me the things I needed to do to get business, how to do marketing, and the strategies that were working. I trusted them. That's significant... if you can find a mentor you trust, and you can just do what they say, exactly the way they say to do it, the process works.

Overcoming those challenges changed my life completely in a lot of different ways. Obviously, a significant result was the marketing that made the phone ring. When you learn a way that works, and you do it over and over again, marketing almost goes on autopilot.

One of the marketing systems I put in place was building a team. That was huge for me—learning to trust people who I did not think could do it as well as I could. However, that has been a significant factor in growing our business. I'm only one person so my time is limited physically at a certain point. Having a team ensures our clients are served well and in a timely way.

Everybody connects with different people so I might not be everyone's cup of tea. By growing a team and trusting my people, not every client has to work with me—they can work with my loan officer assistant (LOA) or my processor. I have so many people now there's likely someone to fit every kind of personality. In this business, that's important. Realtors and loan officers are both salespeople and, sometimes, those personalities clash. By trusting other people and building a big enough team, we are able to match clients with team members by personality. That has helped us grow our business tremendously.

Overcoming Challenges Leads to Self-Confidence

If I could go back in time to ten years ago, the advice I would give myself would be, 'You *can* do this on your own.' For a long time, I had a business partner who I thought was the best at everything. I believed he knew more than me, that he had more business sense than me, and that he had better expertise than me. Over time, and with a lot of insight from my coaching, my confidence grew.

In 2010, it was still really rough in the mortgage business, especially as we were still heavily a refinancing business. I didn't think I could do it by myself. Fast forward to 2019, my partner and I parted ways and I was scared again—I feared I couldn't do it on my own. I thought I needed my now ex-partner to be successful.

However, every month has been a better month than we've ever had, and we've done that without my ex-partner. Even more, we've done it with my leadership. No one else on my team has been in the mortgage business so I know they're succeeding and closing loans because I taught them how to do it. That has been very empowering for me.

I think self-confidence is a big problem for a lot of us. We come into this business, someone takes us under their wing, and then we think we can't do it without them. That is just not true. If you can build referral business in this industry, you can absolutely run it on your own. You have to believe in yourself, however, it's easy to fall back into self-doubt. Every day I have to tell myself to believe in my capabilities because challenges still come up, but I always figure it out.

A lack of self-confidence is something everyone struggles with, whether or not they're in the mortgage business. In business, you cannot let self-doubt stop you. Having confidence does not mean always knowing the answers. Instead, it means knowing you can, and will, figure them out as you go. Without self-confidence, you couldn't get in the car to drive anywhere—you would be too afraid of what you might encounter on the road. And yet, every day drivers get into their cars without realizing the confidence it takes to do it. That kind of knowingness is self-confidence.

Your challenges will be the best things that ever happen to you. That sounds completely counterintuitive but, as I look back over my life, the things I thought would be the end of me were the very things that molded me and made me into who I am today. If you can remember that during challenging times, you will be so much better off. We all face challenges, and many people let those challenges define them. Personally, I choose to let them build me into a stronger, more resilient, and more capable person.

One of the most profound challenges I have faced is the loss of people who were close to me and on whom I deeply depended. Looking back, even though it was super-hard and I miss that person daily even now, it made me more responsible. It made me have to learn how to do things on my own. While I would do anything to go back and have more time with each of those people, I know the experience of their loss shaped me into being an independent businessperson today. Their role model-ship changed my life for the better...maybe that is their legacy.

Another helpful insight I learned that is specific to the mortgage industry is you are not defined by the company where you work. Lots of people tie their identity to their employer when, in reality, people are doing business with *you* in your market. They don't care if it's ABC Mortgage Company. They care that it's Jen Conley or John Smith.

I've been at my current company for quite a while but, previously, I changed companies every couple of years. I've seen first-hand how relationships go with the loan officer vs. a company name. People get so tied up in being part of ABC Mortgage Company but the company is not who people are dealing with—they're calling the loan officer, just like they were calling me. My clients don't trust my company—they trust me. If you can get out of that headspace and realize you are your own little company inside an employer company, and that your own branding of you is more important than your branding of your employer, then your business will flourish.

Do What You Feel Is Right

You might think it's hard to know the impact of a particular strategy, especially when in a new coaching program that will jumpstart your marketing activities. When you're trying a lot of different tactics, it can be hard to tell what is actually working. In my business, we track our progress and results. We know that, while realtor referrals and past database marketing are about half of our business, old-school radio advertising is the other half.

Radio has been a huge outreach strategy to not only get our name out there but, over the years of me doing it, people feel like they know me and like I'm their friend. My voice is with them in the car, at home, or at work. Since they hear me every single day in their own environment, they trust me. Radio ads also help with realtor referrals because there is a perception of consistency and credibility. Borrowers will say, "Oh, I've heard them on the radio." That has been a winning, although maybe unconventional, marketing strategy for us.

As a side note, another small strategy many people don't think about is getting their phone number as a website URL. For instance, if your phone number is 727-787-2275, get the URL of 7277872275.com

It might be because of our radio advertising but people do find us through tracking our phone number in a Google search. I like trying new things to be seen so that's a tip I offer other loan officers.

Another key element in our success, which I alluded to earlier, is our team. The secret to building our team has been transparent honesty, which is the key to everything. When we interview people, we are very honest about who we are, and we ask and expect them to be very honest about who they are as well. When we're in an interview, we put it right out there. We let them know that team members tease each other. We're a family. We have a lot of fun in our office. With that in mind, I need each candidate to be who they are in this interview because, in 90 days, if they turn out to be someone else, it's going to be a problem.

When we started taking that approach in our interviews, people tended to let their guard down so we could see if they were really a good fit or not. It's possible to teach anybody the mechanics of this business, but I can't teach someone to fit into our culture or be someone we want to spend the majority of our waking hours with…and we have to see that upfront in the interview. Everybody's got their Sunday best on in an interview; we encourage and support them in being themselves. By being honest about who we are and allowing them to be honest about who they are, we have built a great team who enjoys coming into work every day.

The mechanics of this business are the processes, the systems, the protocols—and anybody can learn to do them. But if a particular team member doesn't fit, it just makes everybody miserable. We've had those people. It's tough enough to be cohesive and have each other's back, but when you've got that one person who nobody can get along with in the mix, it makes the workday that much harder. Of course, we have ups and downs—we are a family and we have fits and fights—but overall, it's a cohesive group. That team cohesion, that fit, that clarity, started because of the honesty shared in the interview process.

The very first person we tried this honest interview approach with was the proof of how it works. We sat down together and she was sitting up ramrod straight—very prim and proper. We said, "Okay, this is who we are. We make fun of each other. We have a lot of fun." We told her the complete truth and said, "We need you to be who you are because, in 90 days, when you're somebody else, we're probably going to terminate you. So, today, we need to make sure you're the right person." You could see those ideas just wash over her. She relaxed, got bubbly, and wasn't trying to put on this show. We hired her and she's one of my best employees. We haven't had to get rid of anyone or cut a single person after we started interviewing that way because we knew who they were upfront.

I have worked with a coach and a mentor along the way, people who are now lifelong friends. Carl White and Tammy Schneider have changed the face of my business. A lot of people come in and out of your life…but they are a constant for me. They have been in my life for ten years now. It's probably worked so well for me because they cared about me, not about my money. Here's a good example of what I mean by that—I will never forget how this rolled out. There were times early on in coaching where Carl would host an event. I said, "I can't come. My pipeline is not full enough. I can't afford the money. I can't come." Carl said, "You need to be here. That's why you need to be here." Then he offered to pay for me to come. I said, "No, I have to stay here." He said, "Okay, but I better see it in your pipeline."

While Carl is one of the sweetest people and nicest guys you will ever meet, he will hold you accountable. And he did that with me— he followed through. He said, "If you're not going to come and, instead, you're going to stay home, I better see it in your pipeline." That pushed me to work harder because I wanted to show him I was serious about it.

You need a friend, a mentor, somebody, to see what you're doing and pat you on the back and let you know you're doing a good job. But sometimes you also need somebody to have honest conversations with you, always out of love and respect—but with honesty. "You know, Sis, there may be an easier way to do all this." Carl has been that person for me. Finding that quality, that connection, that level of caring in a coach or mentor is integral to growing your business and your life.

The Oddly Profound Power of Saving Money

When I started coaching with Carl, he had a specific plan laid out for loan officers to work. Part of that plan was saving money. Interestingly, a lot of people in the business don't save money and, in the past, that included me. I was never a saver—even before I was in the mortgage business. Every two weeks, he would ask, "Did you start your savings account?" Every time, I would answer, "Oh, I'm going to do it next week…I'm going to do it next week." Finally, he said, "If you don't start your savings account, I'm not going to continue to coach you because you're not taking it seriously." I thought, "Oof, I better do it." So I went and started a savings account. In short order, I almost became addicted to saving money! When you do something like that as a result of a mentor's leadership, it changes the rest of your life.

When you've got that money in savings, it doesn't matter if any one deal closes or not. You don't feel that pressure of trying to close any particular deal because you've got a backup plan in your savings account. I'm not worried about what happens in the market because I've got that backup savings account. When you find someone who cares about you enough to pour what you need to know right in front of you, and who gives you that hard talk when you need it because they love you, it's a whole 'nuther level. Your business (and life) cannot help but change.

Carl does the accountability piece in such a nice way. I am a 'crack the whip' kind of person but that's not necessarily what I need from my coach. Carl does accountability in a way where I don't even realize he's doing it sometimes. For example, a person's relationship with money is conditioned by many life occurrences; for me, my dad was a barber and mom didn't work outside the home. We weren't poor by any stretch, but they never had savings. I watched my dad work until the day he died. He paid ridiculous amounts of life insurance when he was sick so my mom would have money later. Even that wasn't enough to motivate me to start a savings account. But Carl pushing me to do it changed my perspective.

In addition to saving, I bought a house and paid it off in 22 months because I didn't want to have that debt. Savings is a life changer. It's a business changer. People don't realize savings can relieve a lot of pressure on a business. When that relentless and crushing pressure of needing every loan to close is gone, it frees you up to simply go find the next one. You're not trying to beat a square peg into a round hole because you need that loan to close. It's okay…you can still pay your mortgage and buy groceries and gas for your car. You can pursue new opportunities. You don't need to stress. Savings frees you up mentally and emotionally so you can continuously do your best. There is a special power in savings that people don't realize until they try it. I probably still wouldn't have savings without him pushing me to do it, to be quite honest. Like most other mortgage people, I would have just continued to make good money and spend it right away.

Something else that has worked out very well for me is that my business has created a way to bring my family to work with me. My son has worked for me for more than four years now and, for the last two years, he's been our head processor. That has enabled me to work with him every single day. He's my oldest son and it's really great to have that connection with him. Sometimes children grow up, move out, get their own life, get their own job, but I still get to see him every single day.

I have always been really close with both of my kids. His friend group always migrated to our house when they were younger as their hangout spot. I liked that because I knew what they were doing, where they were, and that they were safe. That is relevant to my business today because I have also been able to hire his best friend as his processing assistant. Another woman they grew up with and went to school with is my Loan Officer Assistant (LOA). My son's girlfriend also works for me as my marketing assistant. It is amazing that I have been able to build this whole family team. I get to watch them grow and flourish. And it's just as amazing for them because they are doing something meaningful.

The mortgage business is something that doesn't get enough credit for being a life-changer for people. I've had so many stories of how people who worked for me got to buy their own home and achieve their dreams. Working in our office changed the rest of their life. What we do in this business is really important and sometimes we lose sight of that. Bringing all these extended family members into the business, letting them be part of it, and knowing they're growing a career for the long term is very gratifying. Eventually, when I decide I want to put myself out to pasture, they can take the business and can run it. They can grow it and have a great life too.

By the way, my kids are super savers. Actually, everybody in my office is a good saver but both of my kids are both super savers. My youngest one still lives at home. He wants to move out, but he said he's not moving until he has $10,000. Now, we live in a really small town where monthly rents are about $500. He met his goal and started looking for an apartment but had trouble finding a spot. The good news is his savings account is just growing while he's looking . . . it's around $12,000 now. I'm so thankful my kids don't feel the pressure of self-sacrifice to make just any deal work or like they have to do anything urgent because they need money. That burden makes you miserable. My kids have goals and they want to meet them but it's not a 'this-has-to-close' moment day after day. We've had people who work for us who have been in that place, where they have to get their bonus or they can't pay their bills, and it's rough. Nobody in our office is living like that now—it's a great way to live.

The Realities of Small-Town Business

Over the next few years, I want to continue growing our team, not necessarily locally, although maybe locally for operations. I want to help other loan officers realize they can do this business success-fully too. This is a plan within a system that works and which any-body can do if they plug into it and just do it.

People ask me, "Does coaching work?" Yes, coaching works— IF you do what they tell you to do. That's how this business is too— it works when we work our systems. At this point, we've got such a good team that the business just hums along. I do the marketing and I make sure the phone rings but the everyday tasks and rou-tines are handled by the team. That also allows me to be available to mentor other loan officers. My goal is to bring more loan officers onto our team, which will eventually grow our operational staff as well.

There are so many loan officers who are out there on an island by themselves, going it solo. I've been there myself. Despite all the relationships needed to make this business work, it can be a really lonely business and it doesn't have to be . . . that's a choice. While I can feel like coaching this group of people in this business is really big, it's not—it's a few hundred people. There are thousands and thousands of loan officers who have never heard of our coaching group, or who are doing their business a particular way without knowing there are options, or who haven't heard of me (yet). When I take the time to reach out and find those people to help them grow their business, their life will change. That's just one more thing that will make me a happy camper in a couple of years.

If you live in "Small-Town" USA, here's my advice. Our business is located in a small town of just 22,000 residents. It's a different set of challenges from doing business in a big city.

There are people who think it's so much easier to do business in a small town and that's not necessarily true. It can actually be more challenging. I've heard it all: you've got less competition in a small town, you don't have to fight with hundreds of lenders, that everyone is so nice. However, while it's true there are fewer competitors here locally, I still have online competitors. I may only have eight or nine local competitors, but that means I only have about an eighth of the deals available out of the pool of total loans. In a bigger town, loan officers don't deal with that limitation.

Word also spreads very quickly in this business and even quicker in a small town, which is an added pressure. If we make a mistake, then everybody's going to know it. If I upset one realtor, the other 199 know it by the end of the day. There are times when I have focused on that too much—Carl has helped me get past this particular mental rut as well. I've learned not everybody's thinking about me or my business all the time. It's challenging to remember it doesn't really matter in the end when a day has been particularly tough. Whatever happens that day can sometimes feel like it's the end of the world, but tomorrow nobody's going to remember it. People have short attention spans.

If I had thousands of realtors to build relationships with, I wouldn't stress about something taking a little bit longer, or a condition I have to get, or somebody complaining. Who would hear it in such an ocean of people? However, when you have only 200 realtors, of which only a quarter of those are full-time, with 150 to 180 deals a month closing on average total, that's a whole different set of challenges that bigger city professionals don't have to navigate. If you've got thousands and thousands of realtors to constantly call and generate business with and build new relationships, you don't have that kind of concern. In a small town, we just don't have that option so if you screw up big-time, it can ruin your business quickly.

In the end, the formula for success is simple: focus on good service, preserve your reputation, be honest, show up, do what you know is right, hire an amazing team and follow through with people. Oh, and get into a coaching program. These are the ingredients of solid business growth. Then trust yourself and your people—that's the investment that will pay you back every time.

About Jennifer Conley

I have been in the mortgage industry for 15 years and have learned a lot about the industry and how to help put our customers in the best financial position during that time.

As much as I love the industry and the business, I love working with people the most. There is no greater reward for me than working with someone looking to buy their perfect home and making their dreams come true by finding a way to make their loan work. I've made lifelong friends that started as customers who I helped find a way to save money by refinancing their existing mortgage to help consolidate their debt or cash out equity in their homes.

People. That's what all this is about and I've been so fortunate to work with an unbelievably talented team that takes so much pride in what they do and how they do it. They know that "people" is the reason we get to do what we do.

Over the years, I've found my business is an incredible vehicle for me to make a difference in the world. Four years ago, I started working closely with a 501c(3) organization called Mission Firefly. This ministry works in Central America to install water filtration systems to villages that literally have no power or clean water. This Mayan region is covered in a blanket of poverty. I found my heart for giving in Guatemala, where I've helped establish over 40 clean water filtration systems that provide clean water for more than 40,000 Guatemalans daily. I enjoy traveling down to the region a couple of times a year and watching the kids grow and know that my business, thanks to my team and my clients, has helped these people.

When I go home at night, I get to see my wonderful husband of 27 years and spend time with my two kids and my crazy dogs. I've been a Pug lover for years and have recently added a French Bulldog, Freddie, to the family. Freddie comes to work with me daily and loves warm hugs!

Jennifer can be reached at:

Email: **jen51394@gmail.com**

Phone: 740-708-3245

Website: **jenconley.com** | **8514760.com**

LinkedIn: **linkedin.com/in/jennifer-conley-a94244b/**

Give to Others,
Then Go Be a Mermaid

By Suzanne Downs
Broker Owner
Palm Beach Mortgage Group

When I was young, I loved helping people and decided becoming a nurse would help me do just that. So in my junior year of high school, I became a nurse's aide. I've always been pretty driven so, the following year, I joined the Diversified Career and Technology (DCT) on-the-job training program and became the vice president of it. I worked two jobs, one as a cashier and the other as a nurse's aide at the local hospital.

Upon graduating high school, I took courses at the local University to become a registered nurse (RN). I needed extra money for books and tuition, etc. so I got a job as a receptionist at a mortgage company. Very quickly, I discovered I had a knack for sales and I thought, "I can do this!" Within six months, I got my license and have been slinging mortgages since.

My motivation in life has always been to help people. I started out wanting to help people with their health and ended up helping people with their dreams of home ownership.

Being in the industry for more than 30 years, I have seen a lot. We've been through several refi booms and just about every different market you can imagine; the hardest has to have been in 2007–2008. That was downright hard! Florida was one of the hardest hit markets.

I feel extremely blessed to be able to say that, through hard work and dedication, my team and I have been able to weather the storms and keep the business alive. Even when others were going out of business, we did what we had to do to make it. One of our most significant staying powers is our business model—working with real estate agent referral partners vs. chasing low-rate refi business. We have several long-standing relationships that have stood the test of time.

Another thing that helped us make it through the 2007 Crash was me being willing to take a second job and work extra to pay the bills and keep the doors open. I'm a friendly person by nature and I love to cook and entertain. So, armed with these qualities, I started a catering company. A friend and I started the company with our two kitchens and our two double ovens. With my ability to sell, I landed us some pretty sweet jobs.

Grand openings were one of our specialties. When businesses moved into Palm Beach County, many times we were called to cater. We did openings for hospitals, universities, and we even catered some large weddings. It's probably one of the hardest things I've ever done. While the mortgage business can be stressful, catering takes a toll on your body. But running both of those businesses allowed me to keep going without going into debt.

No Negativity, Only Creativity

As we emerged from the crash in 2010, I put the catering business aside to concentrate on the mortgage business. While many around me seemed to focus on the negative, I focused on the positive. I put a sign on my door that said "no negativity zone." I also turned off my television and stopped watching the news. To this day, I have no clue what's happening in the news.

In addition, I amped up my visits with my referral partners. If they didn't have an interest in pulling themselves out of their black pit of despair, I kindly let the relationship go.

Once the dust settled, I ended up with a core group of three or four agents and knew I needed to get more to grow my business. I put a plan together for snagging agents. Every morning I showed up—I got dressed, got in my car, and drove around town knocking on real estate doors. My strategy was to concentrate on "mom and pop shops," hoping I could convince them to refer all their buyers to me. One thing led to another and I ended up at one of the largest shops in town—Keller Williams. The broker liked me and introduced me to several of their mega teams. I started working with most of them. At the same time, I also became an in-house lender for another local real estate office.

My business grew quickly. My mentor, Carl White, calls this the "pay to play" strategy. This is where a loan officer pays for desk space at a real estate office. And I paid quite a bit! However, Carl also says you have to write little checks to cash big ones. The first check should be an expense, and every check after that should provide a return on the investment. My investment paid off in spades. The busier I got, the more people I needed to hire to service my business. I leveraged myself by hiring loan officers to manage each of the offices.

In 2010, I was upgrading my business and, at the same time, rebuilding my personal life. I had a baby at age 40. I got a divorce and became a single mother to four daughters. It was a crazy time. Despite everything happening around me, I knew I couldn't let my daughters down so I worked my butt off.

In 2013, I received a phone call from The Mortgage Marketing Animals. Somehow, they had heard about my "pay to play strategy" and wanted to hear more about it. I was invited to attend a mastermind meeting in Clearwater, Florida, to share my success. I accepted the invitation and went to that meeting.

It was a small group of about twelve of us. Everyone in the room took turns sharing what they were doing to create success in their business. Even though I'm a great salesperson, I am not a public speaker. When it got close to my turn, my face, chest and neck were beet-red and I felt like I was going to pass out. But I got through it and, even more, felt accomplished when I realized I had done something no one else in the group had achieved.

At the end of the group-share, we did some collective whiteboarding together and mapped out our next 90 days. As Carl worked with me, he asked me to share the one thing I wished I could accomplish. Without hesitation, I said I wished I could spend more time with my daughters. And then I started to cry.

I had missed a lot of time with my girls because I was working so much. As a result of this mastermind meeting, I was able to restructure my team and come up with a plan to hire more people. It was then I vowed I would take a vacation every month, even if it were only three or four days. It's been almost eight years since I made that promise—I've missed it maybe twice since. Which means out of the last 96 months or so, I have literally taken a vacation in about 94 of those months, while drastically increasing my closings. That meeting changed my life and the life of my girls . . . they got their mommy back.

In addition to my time freedom, that meeting also catalyzed me in growing my business and gaining financial freedom. I've taken my daughters on trips all over the world—Hawaii, England, Ireland, Scotland, France, Italy, Belize, and several cruises. My house and a second investment property are both almost paid off. That kind of freedom feels really good.

Give Yourself Credit

If I could go back ten years and talk to myself then, I know exactly what I would say. First, I would encourage myself to pick a word or phrase of the year to set my intentions and focus. I would also tell myself to build my team sooner as a way to leverage myself. And I would also say to give myself a break.

As someone who is extremely driven, I can be hard on myself and don't acknowledge all I have accomplished. I think many people get stuck in comparing themselves to others; instead of looking at how far we've come, we look at others and judge how far we have to go based on their results. The reality is that everyone is on their unique journey and comparison does not support forward progression in our own journey (or theirs).

I continue to recognize and overcome this penchant for comparison in my personal life as well. For instance, as soon as I finished a really hard workout recently, I caught myself saying "you have to stop eating so much and work out even harder." I'm fairly sure my younger self would tell my older (now) self to be compassionate and give myself credit for my accomplishment(s). I once heard we would never talk to other people the way we talk to ourselves; monitor your self-talk to make sure it's positive every day.

In terms of comparison, I love the thought of being in competition only with myself. Am I a better person today than I was yesterday? Am I a little further ahead of the game than I was yesterday? If the answer is yes, I keep going.

If my now-self could go back and sit with my younger self, I would tell myself thank you for being a saver. In our industry, we can make a lot of money. One of the things that helped me make it through the crash was that I did have some savings. That allowed me to start the catering business and get through the hard times. So my advice to others would be to save money, even when you aren't sure you have the bandwidth to do it.

My mentor, Carl, gives a statistic that 78% of NFL football players file for bankruptcy within five years after they retire because no one ever taught them to save. I have made a vow to not overspend and to save and invest as much as I can for the future. One of the things I admire most about our coaching group is that they focus on the future and on creating a legacy and financial freedom.

No Magic Bullet

I have found there is no magic bullet, no single strategy that creates success. Instead, success is a culmination of everything you do consistently on a daily basis. It boils down to focused work on the right things.

There are lots of great strategies and implementation tools you can use to streamline your business processes and systems. My favorite tool of all is old-school—the telephone. Nothing replaces a personal telephone call. I love making those connections on a daily basis and asking for the business.

I've trained several loan officers to be successful. The one thing I see that works consistently is phone calls. Without fail, all my students have had an "A-ha" moment when they come to me and say "oh my gosh, it worked!—I made my calls and got a referral!" So another bit of advice I would give to others is to get over the fear of the telephone. Once I discovered that "no" wouldn't kill me, my life changed for the better—and I've seen that in the loan officers I've trained over the years as well.

In addition to the telephone, I would say hiring a team has made the biggest difference in my business. It's also been one of my biggest challenges.

As a business owner, hiring and retaining a 'unicorn' team has been difficult. It's taken me many years to get to where I am today. As a result, corporate culture is a huge priority for us. I've created a culture in my business that rings of a small family. We care about each other and back each other up every day. We go to each other's birthday parties, hang out on the weekend, and celebrate holidays together. I am from the school of immense gratitude. I am grateful for everyone who works for me. I don't see myself as a "boss"; I just roll up my sleeves and work right next to them.

Sometimes, that family culture does not serve me well. I find it difficult at times to hold people accountable and to implement more efficient systems and processes. However, whatever I am doing seems to be working and my team is stronger and happier than ever.

It's Ok to Cry

I've been told my heart is three sizes too big. I suppose I am the opposite of the Grinch. And given that, in the past, the mortgage business has traditionally been a male-dominated business, (although that is changing now as our business has evolved), it's been interesting to be a heart-driven woman in this arena. There have been many times I have cried because of something that happened—but that doesn't mean I stop. For me, it's a pressure release for stress. I don't consider it a weakness; instead, crying is how I deal with the stress and get back to center so I can move forward again.

A year and a half ago, when I first started dating my fiancé (a man I've known for 30+ years), he asked me, "do you cry a lot?" I replied, "I don't think so but let me ask my friends." Everyone responded with a resounding "yes!" So now I simply acknowledge it is part of who I am. Actually, I'm proud I have not let my heart get hard after everything I have experienced. My advice to anyone would be to live your life to its fullest, give to those around you, and don't be afraid to show your emotions.

The Difference

The single biggest thing I can attribute to my success (besides hard work) is coaching. I think everyone should have a mentor or coach. I chose to align myself with Carl White, Tammy Schneider and the

Freedom Club. I've worked with several of the coaches and each has been an amazing experience. Personally, I don't do it for the accountability piece because I am so driven, I don't need that. However, I do need advice, support, and to surround myself with other people who have the same dreams and desires as I do.

It's not just what I've learned that has been so rewarding. It is also the relationships I have formed with other members of the group. Many of us speak daily and a group of us even vacation together. I love the sense of belonging and family I experience with the Freedom Club. It's amazing to be part of a group that shares an abundance mentality and who invite positivity into their lives. The members of this group are among the most generous, inspiring, and insightful people I've met. I don't think you can put a price tag on being part of a coaching family and having a coach.

Carl always says, "you need a place where you can spike the ball." In the group, we celebrate when another member joins the "2 Comma Club." This means that yet another member is now making over $1,000,000 as personal income so we celebrate that victory with them. Sometimes we can't share with those around us the income we make so it's nice to have a place to share, feel inspired, and inspire others.

Giving Back Is Going Forward

Helping others is a theme that runs through my business. Whether I'm helping a new person get started in our business, helping a client get into a home, or I am helping my referral partners grow their business, I love helping.

One of the things I believe has led to my great success is finding people outside of our industry and training them up. Most of my team are people I trained from scratch. I love creating a relationship with someone and helping them turn their life around. For me, this creates loyalty and everyone on the team is inspired to help me grow my business. I have found, more often than not, they almost want it more than I do. They are in it for my success as well as their own.

As corny as it sounds, I still get really excited about helping someone achieve home ownership. It's the biggest financial transaction a person typically makes in life. I genuinely want to help people experience that dream so my team and I will do whatever it takes to make it happen for them. There have been many times where I have helped people who have been told "no" when trying to buy a home. Most of the time, someone just didn't want to be bothered with going the extra mile to help them.

With our experience, we can usually figure out even the toughest of deals. Helping people become first-time home buyers is extremely gratifying to me. Giving back to help someone go forward fills a special place in my heart.

Make Time to Be a Mermaid

The older I get, the more I think about where I want to be in a few years. My first answer is "the beach." There is something about the water, sun, and sand that just does something for me. Recently, my best friend surprised me with a trip to St. John where we met a professional photographer on a beach and did a mermaid shoot. It was the experience of a lifetime. I kept the tail. Now whenever I need a pick-me-up, I hit the water and swim. I highly recommend finding something that feeds your soul and brings joy. Make time to rejuvenate to feel and perform at your best.

One of the things I've learned over the years is that you have to like yourself. You really have to like who you are inside and live congruently with that person. This insight has served me well. I try to make something happy or fun out of everything I do.

My goal in the next five years is to position myself so I can sell my business. That never crossed my mind prior to joining the Freedom Club. Like many loan officers, I was a one-man band, working 12-hour days with no value in the business because, without me, there was nothing. Now, I have a sellable business. I am going to continue to grow my team, perfect my realtor partner relationships, and implement systems and processes so I am ready to sell when the time is right.

I don't see myself ever really quitting. What I love about our business is we can do it part-time if we choose and from anywhere in the world. Even after I sell, I will probably continue to do one or two loans a month. For now, I will continue the hard work for the next several years with that end goal in mind. That and getting married in a castle in Ireland.

I say that with a light heart but, in all seriousness, it's important to believe in what you want and to put it out there. Be optimistic! I love spreading that kind of positivity and inspiration to others. My life word is believe. I have it everywhere—on plaques in my house, in my office, and even engraved on my jewelry. It's everywhere I look because everything you do—every thought, every action, every outcome, every dream—depends on believing in it 100%.

In closing, my advice is to write down what you want; dream big and then hire a coach to help you make it happen.

About Suzanne Downs

Suzanne Downs has been originating home loans since 1985 and established Palm Beach Mortgage Group, Inc. (as a Co-Owner & Founder) in 2001.

Previously, Suzanne served as President of the Florida Association of Mortgage Brokers where she currently serves the organization as a Local Chapter Director.

Suzanne is a leader and trained specialist in the mortgage industry. Currently, the business belongs to the Florida Association of Mortgage Brokers, the Palm Beach Chamber of Commerce, and the Better Business Bureau. They offer competitive rates, renowned customer service, satisfaction, and a variety of programs to meet specific lending needs, i.e.: CONVENTIONAL, FHA/VA, JUMBO, NON-CONFORMING and NO DOC programs.

Suzanne can be reached at:

Email: **sdowns@palmbeachmortgagegroup.com**

Phone: 561-714-4605

Website: **palmbeachmortgagegroup.com**

Facebook: **facebook.com/Palm-Beach-Mortgage-Group-Suzanne-Downs-155972311110418**

LinkedIn: **linkedin.com/in/suzannedowns/**

Push Past the Fear—Keep Going

By Robert Fillyaw
Southeastern Area Manager
AnnieMac Home Mortgage

I was burnt out. I was managing a branch for Bank of America (B of A), with 15 or 16 employees, and was also in the Marine Corps Reserve. I was burnt out on managing people and having my pay-check dependent on other people and their actions and activities, or lack thereof. I was burned out on the lack of time flexibility in my schedule—working in that retail bank was like a ball and chain. I had to be there at 8:30 A.M., had 20 minutes for lunch, and didn't make my day-end escape until 5:30 or 6:00 P.M.—there was no flex-ibility even to run an errand. I didn't have a lot of control. I didn't have a lot of autonomy or entrepreneurial creativity or capability in that role.

Then I got activated to deploy to Iraq in 2005. I supported Oper-ation Iraqi Freedom in the desert for a year and seven months. I was a squad leader, managing and leading Marines in a combat zone. I came back in October of 2006 because I was getting married in December. I looked at my soon-to-be wife, and I said, "I don't want to go back to managing people, managing a branch, and not having at least some flexibility or more control. I'm going to go be a loan officer where I can be in charge of me and have a little bit more flexibility. Maybe I can build and grow a business within a company. And maybe money will be a little bit better as well." That life pivot is what pushed me into full-time mortgage origination.

Some of the biggest challenges I've faced have been things beyond my control. Twice, I've been at a company that either merged with or acquired another company; virtually overnight, my entire world would change. That means the way we did business, the policies, the procedures—everything changed. Both of those times led to a transition away from those companies into a new company. That's always challenging because it's unexpected—you don't see that coming and there's no control over the events as they unfold. I remember when Bank of America purchased Country-wide. Even though we purchased Countrywide, the mortgage department turned into Countrywide. I literally went home on Friday with B of A, came back on Monday with Countrywide—and my whole world had changed in terms of how we did business and what kind of business we could do.

Back then, in 2010, closing a million dollars in loan volume a month was a good month for me. I remember packaging $1.2 million dollars in loans on a Friday that, when I returned that next Monday, were not able to be done. I put them in a FedEx box and sent them to another originator. My days with B of A were numbered after I put those files in that box. That taught me I'm an adaptor.

Challenges Forced Positive Change

Overcoming those challenges was all about taking action. I had to find a new company that would support me and give me the ability to go to the next level. As I look back on my career, every move, every step, everything that's happened I know—definitively—has happened for a reason. I wouldn't be here today with the team I have and the business we're doing if it weren't for those experiences—even Bank of America. So the transitions were good. They kicked me out of my comfort zone and forced change, adaptation, and finding the right path for me at the time.

Overcoming those challenges was tough because each was a curveball I didn't see coming. It redefined what I was looking for in a company partner, then going out and having the conversations to find that right fit. I can't even say the end result of it all has happened yet because life is still happening; however, every one of those catalysts moved me further along on my journey to growing that entrepreneurial business within a business and yearning for autonomy.

Because of those transitions, when I set out to open my own branch, and to run my own profit and loss center, I had a clear and defined idea of what I was looking for in that role. That clarity has put me where we're at now. If those things hadn't happened, and if I hadn't had to overcome those challenges, I would still be a single loan officer, a one-man band trying to produce as much business in volume as possible. I would not have taken the steps to grow and build what I've built, which is now a team that handles my production, then moved on to the next level of having a region with multiple loan officers in multiple locations. Currently, I have ten branches in five states. We are going to do about $300 million in production this year. That's a long way from 2010 when I was doing $18 million in production for the entire year as a single loan officer.

Building to Billions

The goal for my team is to be at one billion in the next five years—we're pushing hard for it and I believe we'll hit that target. On a personal level, what I do now is much more rewarding and fulfilling than any ability or potential I had as a single loan officer. I'm literally able to find loan officers who are in broken systems, who don't have the team support, who don't know how to grow their business, who don't have the leadership or the guidance within the companies they're with so I can help them. We're talking to someone right now who knows exactly what they need to do but the company they're at just won't allow them. The company won't give them the ability to do it. I have the structure that gives them that autonomy to grow their success.

Bringing those loan officers in and, honestly, changing their lives by helping grow their business through taking their production from $6 million to $20 million in a year has a real impact on their life and their families. It's pretty special. For me, personally, there's a lot more satisfaction and fulfillment in that. My wife would also tell you that my work schedule is not quite as stressful. When you've got a team and people who you can count on and trust versus trying to do it all on your own, it reduces the stress level and the workload while increasing the income.

In the next five years, our goal is to have my group, The More Mortgage Group at AnnieMac, at $1 billion dollars of production. How are we going to get there? We foresee a two-pronged approach path.

The first part of our two-pronged approach is through talent acquisition and recruitment, which is great because that's a powerful shift for me and where I get a lot of fulfillment. At first, it was about originating for me, but then it became about building a team, then building the branch, then getting the leadership and support in place. Now the ship is built. It's time to launch it, fill it up, and take people on the ride. I'm shifting gears to recruiting with a heavy, strong focus on finding those loan officers—the ones I mentioned who are stuck and having immense challenges and can't grow their business—to bring them in and help them grow.

The second part of our strategy is to, with the loan officers and technology we have alongside the available support, help them grow and up-tier their business. We have found that 82% of the originators we bring in double their business in the first year. It's that two-prong combination of bringing the originator in from recruitment efforts and then giving them the leadership, the guidance, the tools, and the support to grow their business by double or even triple in that first year and beyond that will get us to a billion dollars in the next five years.

Stay Humble, Be Kind

If I could go back to 2010, which was an interesting year for many reasons, not the least of which my twins being born—a boy and a girl, I would tell myself a lot of things. I left Bank of America that year, where I had been for eleven years. I would tell myself to keep going to the gym. I would tell myself to have patience with your children, your wife, your family, and those around you. I would tell myself to be humble and be kind. I would say that, as your business starts growing over the next ten years—and it will!—to stay centered and treat people the right way. If you don't, it'll have lasting negative impacts and unfavorable consequences on you as you try to continue to grow and move forward.

I would tell myself to save money, more than I did, because we were just coming out of a boom and the next few years from 2010 into 2013 were really bleak from an income standpoint. So I would tell myself to not spend as much and save more money. In fact, that's a good message for loan officers right now as we're currently coming off the largest mortgage market in the history of mortgage lending. Loan officers are making more money than ever but they don't have to spend it all, it will keep. You can save money. Do that because we're going to see some market retraction.

I would also tell myself to take risks sooner. I made a couple of career moves that were good and I learned from each of them but, in hindsight, I should have taken this opening-my-own-branch risk sooner than 2018. When I was hit by that last acquisition in 2015, it triggered a need to find a new partner. I should have done the P and L model long ago for my branch but I was scared; I was too risk averse. My overall message would be to push past your fears and keep going.

Push Past Fears and Keep Going

Going further, that would be my message to other loan officers as well—push past your fear and keep going, which is applicable to so many areas of our business. That applies to things like picking up the phone to call that real estate agent or asking for the business. Just a few minutes ago, I had a loan officer in my office who joined us maybe four months ago who has never really marketed or reached out to real estate agents. She didn't really have a plan; no one had shown her what to do or how to do it. That alone can be a game-changer in her business.

In fact, she called to let me know that, just today, she had three coffee appointments with agents who she had called and asked for the meeting. She set the coffee appointment, which is outside her comfort zone. She was sharing with me that those meetings went great, but she was also kicking herself a little bit because, as they were finishing those meetings, that old fear crept in and she didn't ask for the business. So pushing past your fear is applicable in so many different facets of what we do in this business.

The good news is that, even if you let fear hold you back from moving forward today, it doesn't mean that fear can stop you tomorrow. Once you know the pattern, you can identify what's happening in the moment faster so you can handle it differently. We finished the conversation and I said, "Go pick up the phone and call her right now and say, 'Hey, listen, I meant to ask at our coffee appointment ... if you have any buyers to work with, I'd love to work with you in the future. Can I count on you to call me when you have your next buyer lead?'" Push past that fear and keep going.

The second piece of advice for loan officers is to be humble and to be kind—also very applicable in many facets of our business. Don't get too full of yourself.

This is a lesson I had to learn myself. I was cocky, arrogant, and not super great to be around at some points in my career. As my volume started growing and people were giving me accolades, I was just mean. I was acting 'ugly' towards processors and under-writers; I was too full of myself.

One day, I had an eye-opener with someone who I really respected, trusted, and had a lot of admiration for... and they level-set me. They cared enough to tell me I was being a jerk and that I needed to stop that behavior. It opened my eyes and changed my whole perspective. That conversation has had lasting consequences. There are people I know in the market who I would love to realign and do business with but they remember me from 2014 and 2015 when I was kind of a jerk-face meanie. They don't want to entertain any conversations, and I don't blame them. I hold out hope I can redeem those relationships in the future. For now, I focus on the people already in my world and the people I'm going to meet next. A lesson learned: Be Humble!

Ask for the Business

For me, good old-fashioned "asking for the business" has been what's closed the most loans. So many times as loan officers we do all the things we need to do—we make the calls, we go on the appointments, we schmooze, we do the events, we bring the donuts, we attend the closings—we do all of those things. We do it all right. We have great rapport with these agents and the customers, but the business doesn't come. So we sit there and scratch our head and think, 'why, why, why isn't the business here?' The answer is pretty straightforward—it is because we're not asking for it.

We assume that people know we want their business. They might know that but we're not asking for it . . . and you don't get what you don't ask for. The loan agent I mentioned previously with the three coffee appointments said, "Yeah, but they have got to know I want their business." I said, "They probably do, but you didn't ask them for it. So you don't know that she didn't leave and think maybe you don't want to work with her or that maybe you're too busy and you can't take her on." When you ask for the business, it alleviates all of that potential misunderstanding. It gets all of that out of the way and there's no misconception or difference in perception. One of my favorite quotes is, "perception is 90% of reality." What you perceive becomes your reality, whether or not your perception is distorted or unfounded.

So unless you clearly communicate and ask for the business, you don't know what the other person's perception is of you and your business . . . whether you can or can't take them on, whether you're willing or not to take them on, whether or not you like them enough to work with them. But when you ask for the business, it fixes all of that confusion and clears the fog.

I've got a guy in my office who has been in the mortgage industry a long time. He probably got into the mortgage industry in 1996 and has consistently been a $6 to $8 million dollar a year guy. Toward the fourth quarter last year, he came and said, "I want to grow my business and I'm committed. I need to know what I need to do." I said, "Well, you know every agent in town—they all love you. I've long wondered why they aren't sending you business. Are you asking them for the business?" He said, "I'm not." "So let's start there," I said. "Let's do that. Ask for the business." He started asking for their business consistently and with intention. As a result, he's going to close $20 million dollars this year. He went from $6.5 million last year to $20 million the next year, all because he started asking for the business from people. That's probably the biggest piece of advice that's helped me close the most loans...simply asking for the business.

Don't Be Another Salesperson

In terms of team building, one thing to know is that it is hard. You have to be genuine in building your team. When you're talking to people, trying to share your vision, your dream, your goal while getting them to buy into that, to trust you, to upset their life and join you on this journey, it's all for naught if you're not genuine and sincere. When I'm talking to a loan officer, a processor, or an underwriter, whether they're on the team or we're talking to them about joining, I think they can hear the sincerity. They can hear that I'm not blowing smoke and I'm not a guy who is full of crap.

Speaking of which, there's a lot of BS in our business. There are a lot of people who will tell you whatever they think they need to tell you. We're a business made of salespeople—we sell. That's what we do. Salespeople will generally tell you whatever they think they need to so they get your buy-in and bring you over to their product. But that approach is very shortsighted and doesn't lead to relationships. Anything in our businesses that isn't based on a relationship isn't going to last. I've learned it's about being genuine, upfront, honest, sincere, and making sure everyone knows they can count on me, that I've got their back, that what I tell them is what's going to happen. That's a rarity in our industry. It's something we bring to the table in our business and it makes a big difference.

Coaching Is More Than Hipity-Dipity

If I could give only one piece of advice, it would be to get a coach. Working with my mentor has changed my life. If we take a journey back in time to about 2016, I had seen Carl White's ads on Facebook.

I had a working knowledge of who he was, but not a really strong understanding of the bigger picture of his work. I did a strategy planning call that totally blew my mind. Subsequent to that, I signed up with The Freedom Club and the Mortgage Marketing Animals, and started coaching. That was when I started getting intentional about building the team, the systems, the group, and having a business that wasn't one fire to the next but, instead, had a process and a way to do things.

When I started coaching, I was doing around $28–$35 million as a single loan officer, working 70 hours a week. My normal schedule was that I would come into the office around 8:30 or 9:00, work until 6:00, and then go home. I would be with my wife and children until they fell asleep at 8:30 or 9:00. Then I was back on my laptop until 1:00–2:00 A.M. every night. That was six days a week. We'd go on vacation but not plan any activities until usually around 11:00 A.M. or noon because I would work in the morning. We would go out and do an activity or two until 3:00–4:00 P.M., then go back to the hotel room and I would work until dinner. We would go out to dinner and then back to the hotel so I could work. It wasn't a business—it was just me. Coaching enabled me to put some filters and pieces in place. I brought on my first loan officer assistant and started working to build the rest of my team. I stopped being a one-man band. That was a huge change in my life. Fast forward to now and my personal team is going to do well over $100 million this year. I don't take my laptop home. I'm in the office at 9:00 A.M. and leave at 6:00 P.M. and that's it. We go on vacation and I'm checked out. I'm off. I'm really on vacation.

Coaching has enabled me to build a business to run so it is more like I am running a business instead of "working a job." I did individual coaching for a while and then went to the Branch Managers Academy (a division of the Freedom Club) with Kevin Gillespie where I learned a lot of the tools and things I needed to successfully run a branch. It was amazing. I coached with him for a bit and then came full circle by joining The Freedom Club as a coach. Now I coach and mentor loan officers and branch managers across the country through The Freedom Club.

At this point, my personal mentor is Carl White. He and I talk at least once a month and he's always got some nuggets, some piece of advice to give me or a strategy to implement. I recently brought on an in-branch recruiter, who is in my office and does nothing but recruit for our group. That was all Carl's brainchild. He said, "Let me pitch you this idea—what do you think?" And off I ran with it.

Now, as we look back, my wife and I laugh because, when I set the meeting to take that very first call to get introduced to coaching, we were talking about it right before I got on the call. I was saying, "Meh, you know, I just don't know. I don't think this is me. I'm not really into that. I don't do the whole 'new age, hipity-dipity, get-in-touch-with-your-feelings' thing. That's not the person I am. I don't think this is going to be for me." Now, knowing the impact and the change coaching has had on our lives not only from, obviously, an income standpoint but, more importantly, from a quality and a time standpoint, it is evident I really needed the coaching. The difference in time I've had with my children since 2017...there's no price you can put on that.

Gut It to Get It

There are a ton of things that have worked out well for me...I've lived a pretty blessed life. The biggest one right now as it relates to business is getting past my own fears and insecurities about opening my own branch. Anybody reading this—if you get something that's kind of tickling the back of your mind, something you're thinking you want to do to take your business to the next level and you haven't done it because fear is stopping you, jump in!

Opening the branch has worked out really, really well. Of course, it was a struggle at first. We opened the branch in January of 2018, just as market compression hit the mortgage industry. Every pro-forma and projected number we had run through got utterly and completely crushed because margin compression hit and we couldn't hold margin on anything. It was a challenge. There were a number of nights when my wife and I would look at each other and question if it was the right decision. But we stuck it out. We gutted it out. We made it work. And it's worked out extremely well. I'm really excited to see how it continues to grow and where we go with it.

Speaking as someone who has grown a lot through challenges, through coaching, through gutting out the tough times and becoming the person who has a system, a structure, and a growing team of talented people, who has faced deep-seated fears to step into next-level success, who has been where a lot of loan officers are now, I get it. I know what it's like to be a one-man band and I know what it's like to trust my team. The latter is way better.

To get to work with the people in my business today is a privilege. They have choices—they don't have to work in my company. The fact that they do is a blessing to me and, ideally, to them as well. None of it would have happened unless I pushed past my fears—which still come up!—and just kept going. We have a ginormous goal ahead of us and that's going to push some buttons along the way—and it will all be worth it when we reach that goal together.

So just do it—push past your fears and just keep going. When you do, you will be rewarded beyond what you can see every time.

About Robert N. Fillyaw

I am a husband to an amazing woman and father to awesome twins, a boy and a girl. I'm a huge Florida Gator fan, my family and I enjoy football and basketball season very much . . . and we also love to travel! We enjoy visiting new places as well as our favorites, which include St Augustine, Las Vegas, and New York.

On the business side of things I am the Southeastern Area Manager in Gainesville, FL for AnnieMac Home Mortgage and run the #1 group in the company! I am also a mortgage business coach with The Mortgage Marketing Animals Freedom Club . . . I help originators scale their business and build out teams, systems, and processes to increase productivity. I also enjoy real estate investing and flipping houses . . . my wife and I have more than 50 homes to date.

I began in the financial industry in 1999 as a part time teller and worked my way up to be a branch manager. I closed my first mortgage loan in 2003 and decided to jump in full time in 2007. From 2007 through 2017 I focused on growing my personal production and building a team to help my business run smoothly . . . by the end of 2017, I had grown my personal production to $65 million a year with 300+ units. In 2018, I decided to launch my own branch and partnered with AnnieMac Home Mortgage to do so. My group closed about $85 million in 2018, $125 million in 2019, $300 million in 2020 and is pushing to build to a billion a year in funding in the next five years!

My focus is on building the southeast out . . . an area I lovingly refer to as 'the y'all states.' I help loan officers that are in broken systems with little to no support figure out a better way to do business and grow. The average Loan Officer who comes into my group doubles their business within twelve months of doing so and cuts their weekly hours worked by up to 20%. I coach and support on team building and working smarter vs. harder. We have 'best in business' operational support and stellar marketing and technology tools that we provide to help our Loan Officers excel and win in their marketplaces.

I am a member of many boards and associations that focus on real estate including GACAR and BANCF, as well as many local area Chambers of Commerce. I am also a lifetime member of the VFW as I served eight years in the United States Marine Corps and was deployed to Iraq in support of Operation Iraqi Freedom. I have the knowledge, experience and drive to propel your mortgage career to the next level!

Robert can be reached at:

Email: **rfillyaw@annie-mac.com**

Website: **www.annie-mac.com**

Phone: 352-665-1302

Facebook: **facebook.com/RobertFillyawMortgage**

facebook.com/AnnieMac-Home-Mortgage-The-Fillyaw-Team-155108168530532

facebook.com/AnnieMac-Home-Mortgage-Gainesville-1304722789628680

facebook.com/robert.fillyaw

Linkedin: **linkedin.com/in/robertfillyaw/**

The Predictable Growth Plan

By Heath Goodrich and John Hinks, Jr.,
Co-Producing Branch Managers
Lending Path Mortgage

Passion drove both Heath and John into becoming loan officers. John's father established The Hinks Company in June of 1983 when there were very few mortgage lenders in the Columbia market. Before joining the family business, John moved overseas to be a teacher and rugby player. After returning stateside in 2004, John joined his dad in meeting Columbia's mortgage needs.

That was when John realized he needed a different team—a mortgage team. Part of that plan was finding the right partner—enter Heath. Before meeting John, Heath had a job at a finance company that happened to do mortgages as well as personal loans and he loved it. The ability to help a family into a home and realize their dream propelled him to continue down the mortgage path and become a mortgage broker.

In 2011, Heath and John established Lending Path Mortgage. The two concentrated on how to better the mortgage process for their clients while managing the numerous obstacles and regulations required for compliance. The challenges faced when starting out are common—determining how to grow, do more business, and prioritize both focus and resources without working 70 hours a week. Initially, the Lending Path team consisted of only John, Heath, and a processor closing 10–15 loans a month. They managed okay but they did not have a growth plan.

Work the Plan

Developing and following a plan is the most predictable way to successfully grow a business. Overcoming challenges starts by identifying the problem, coming up with a solution, and then implementing that solution. At that time, the two knew they needed to identify, develop, and then implement the right plan for Lending Path to grow, which is what led them to connect with The Freedom Club, Carl White's coaching program.

The coaching program is what Lending Path needed to become the success it is today. The program taught Heath and John the value of a team so their focus could be on the money-making activities required to grow. By joining the program, the two learned that the coaches would help them develop a clear plan for success and, consequently, keep them accountable for implementing that success plan. An additional and unexpected advantage of the program is not only having the support from the coaches but also connecting with others in the group facing the same challenges. In fact, that might be the most valuable part of working with a coaching group—gaining insights and resolution strategies from like-minded people in the business.

One thing is certain for every business—change is crucial to growing it successfully. You have to be open-minded and willing to change the way you operate in order to grow. Change does not mean disregarding the plan; instead, it means analyzing the results and changing the plan based on the desired outcomes. Sometimes growth can mean taking a step back before stepping forward, meaning the way you operate has to change as the business changes. For example, it could mean going from being a micromanager doing everything to becoming someone who hires talented people and lets them help elevate the business. It's a different game plan, a different business model, and requires a different perspective.

Naturally, changing business conditions requires an open mind to a different way of thinking. However, when thinking differently, your values and principles must remain constant. It can be easy to lose sight of those core elements in the excitement of potential growth; you cannot let that happen. It's vital to hold on to what created the foundation of your business as you expand it.

The Daily Success Plan

As long as Heath and John follow their values and principles, work their plan, and do what they believe, everything works out. In John's case, there were times when he could be impatient or see opportunity and have FOMO (the Fear Of Missing Out). That fear can cause restless nights, frustration, or even a sense of going backward because progress is not evident. However, he has learned there are times when momentum means going forward in all directions—even if it looks like going backward for a minute. The best advice is to not force the process—just let it happen. Hold on to your principles and core beliefs around the business. To do anything other than that means compromising self-integrity, risk losing your principles, and forcing growth the hard way.

On the flip side, Heath would counsel on the importance of implementing a plan sooner than later. The pace of growth can slow to be more methodical in approaching any plan. Once you have the plan, dedicate 150% of focus, resources, time, energy, and tasks to implementing that plan. On a micro-level, from a personal production standpoint, an example of a plan is to use a Daily Success Plan (DSP).

Essentially, a DSP is used every day as a guide for your tasks and time investments to grow your business. One focus of such a plan is to spend a dedicated two hours a day working "on" the business (vs. "in" the business) by creating more relationships that bring in more business. As Carl White says, "don't get so busy building the farm that you forget to milk the cows."

Working Harder Together

It takes hard work and dedication to maintain any successful partnership. One challenge is just learning how the other operates and then being able to adequately distribute responsibilities and learn to see eye-to-eye, establishing a solid middle ground that works for both partners. Overall, the pair have the same goals but have different paths in mind to reach them. Identifying those differences enables them to see their weaknesses and lean into the strengths of the other partner.

Acknowledging strengths and weaknesses, in turn, creates a certain role for each partner to balance the other. John became more of the sales manager in helping loan officers grow their business while Heath took on the operations role to ensure the infrastructure was in place to grow. John is more of a big-picture guy while Heath is more strategic in planning the steps to reach that big picture. By honoring their individual strengths, each can play on those and allow the other to do what they are good at while staying in their own lane. Fortunately, their partnership stands after nine years, partially because shared growth opportunities (aka, challenges) have made Heath and John stronger in working through them together.

Flipping the Pyramid

An advantage of Heath and John's partnership and their interpersonal dynamic is that one partner can see five years down the road and the other knows you can't get five years down the road unless you can survive the next three months. Fortunately, that understanding happened organically for Heath and John. Where John looks to expand their horizons beyond what they think today, Heath keeps the pace of their business growth reasonable to protect them from doing a poor job of implementing their growth plan. John has pushed growing the branch size while Heath has slowed the pace just enough to ensure they can still deliver amazing customer service to their loan officers, staff, and clients. To put it plainly, they balance each other out by bringing their different capabilities to the table.

The goal has always been to create a place where loan officers can thrive and have a platform unlike anything they've experienced previously—where they can truly build their business. This is their operational paradigm and working structure from a branch standpoint. From a customer standpoint, Heath and John deliver customer service at a consistent level ten out of ten by having incredibly talented people who are dedicated to supporting the loan officers. That commitment has a trickle-down effect throughout their business from the branch level to all teams and staff members.

Two of their unwritten guiding business principles are authenticity and clear communications. For example, every time they talk about bringing in a new loan officer, they ask themselves, 'can we realistically deliver what we're telling them?' If not, with 100% full transparency, they then say, "We would love to have you join us, but at the moment we can't serve you the way you deserve to be served. Give us the opportunity to get our branch to a point where we can more fully meet your needs and interests."

Another principle is how they approach an infrastructure model. That is, if you were to draw the traditional mortgage pyramid as a model for branch infrastructure, you would put the branch manager at the top, the loan officers in the middle, and the staff at the bottom. Heath and John flipped that model upside down. They reversed that pyramid to put the staff at the top of the pyramid, the loan officer in the middle, and the branch manager at the bottom. Their philosophy, expectation, and plan is that the branch manager works to see what s/he can do to make the loan officers' and operational staff's lives better in this servant leadership model. Every day, leaders and branch managers make sure their staff has the tools and support they need to do their job to its fullest. Their branch leadership does not stop at the basics; instead, they go beyond by also considering and supporting work-life balance, economic freedom, time flexibility, personal empowerment, appreciation for their work, and more. The underlying principle is that they do a particularly good job of taking an average loan officer and, by providing staff and support, turn them into a top-producing loan officer.

The Real Rewards

There are multiple results and rewards that come from overcoming challenges. One such prize is setting production records annually. As a branch, they are closing a volume nearly three times greater than last year's closed business, with the overall increase being ten times from when they started. That kind of production, fueled by hard work, brings more compensation and more provisions for their families and future.

More than that, Heath and John have also built something meaningful through Lending Path. Obviously, the production is powerful because the kind of money the loan officers are making is life-changing. There's also pride in knowing they have 42 people who work with them—not for but with them—who enjoy going to work and love doing their job every single day. Heath and John are proud of establishing a work environment that makes people's lives better. To see their team members' quality of life grow over time inspires and motivates them all over again. Just this one aspect to their business makes all the challenges worth it.

When you put people first, including their desires, goals, and dreams, and you help them achieve what they want, the byproduct is even more production which enriches the company as a whole. The money comes but the true gratification comes from helping and seeing others grow.

Straightforward Success Tips

Plans change, but there always needs to be one to know where you are going. So success tip number one for business growth is to have a written plan, then to live and breathe implementing that plan to bring it to life every day, and invite others to help work it. When you have a goal without a plan, it's like driving to the other side of the country without a roadmap; chances are, you'll never get there. Or if you do, you'll have taken the long way, the trip will take longer, and you will chew through resources in making it happen. It's important to wake up and be motivated every day to achieve your goals.

So number one, have a plan. Number two, implement that plan. Number three, you can't do it alone—you need to build a team to help you achieve your goals. Additionally, have an accountability person who has both the permission and obligation to call you out on achieving your plan. Why? Because if you don't actually act on your plan, you won't make progress.

When investing your time, energy, and resources into growing a business, it's important to realize that exhausting yourself and burning out is possible—even likely. Work-life balance is so much more important than volume and numbers. It is possible to achieve the numbers you want and still get home to spend quality time with your family. The trick is finding that formula, that business plan, which allows you to achieve that because when you avoid burnout, you stay strong and work at peak efficiency.

A profoundly powerful success tip is to always surround yourself with like-minded individuals to keep your game up and to learn from them by letting their experience and perspective guide you. Heath and John had that experience together and also found it with the Freedom Club. The Club is a natural way to be around other individuals who have challenges that are different yet relevant; even more, they can help and learn from each other's experiences. You don't have to reinvent the wheel because people have gone down that path before…utilize their knowledge and resources to learn how to achieve your goals in the most direct way.

They say when you're the smartest person in the room, you are in the wrong room and need to find a new one. As part of The Freedom Club, students attend quarterly meetings and meet others running their businesses and addressing similar challenges. Learning from peers has been priceless because it makes you feel good about yourself—it's not just you having issues. There's some bittersweet relief there. A significant part of their growth and success has come from being around those kinds of people who invite Heath and John to be their best; they experienced that with Carl White's program.

Always Something More to Learn

In terms of coaching, there is absolutely 100% no way Heath and John would be where they are today without the guidance of coaching. The initial benefit of having a coach is having the structure—scheduled meetings to work through the plan while knowing you're committing to creating results. You are putting in the time, energy, and resources, with dedicated focus on implementing an initiative in your business. Second, having that unwavering accountability each and every week is crucial to the building of a real business. To hone your growing edge, invest in coaching and be around others who are investing in coaching as well.

As you grow, you will find coaches in different places beyond the ones you hire. Coaches are around you everywhere. The partners of the company Heath and John work with now have become coaches for them as a matter of course in doing business. The loan officers and operational staff at Lending Path have taught them as well.

Football quarterback Peyton Manning demonstrates his commitment to coaching even to this day. He has hired Coach David Cutcliffe, his Tennessee offensive coordinator who eventually ended up becoming the head coach at Duke University, to work with him. Even when Peyton was in the National Football League (NFL), he still went back to Coach Cutcliffe, his original coach, to get off-season coaching. Some people reminded Peyton he was the best quarterback in the entire league. Then they asked, "Is there another level you can go? Why do you still have your college coach as your coach?" Peyton said, "The day I stop getting coached is probably the day I should stop playing."

There's always something more to learn in life and business. One of the keys is being able to identify who you ask for advice from and who you need to help keep you accountable for your peak performance. Heath and John ascribe to that same philosophy every day in their business.

Secrets in Plain Sight

There are a couple of strategies that stand out which have worked well in closing more loans in their business. One strategy is to just do 'it', no matter what 'it' is—get 'it' done. Do what you can on 'it', even if it's a step vs. the entire project . . . and do it consistently. Whether you're using phone calls, handwritten notes, face-to-face meetings, or text messages for connection, plan out your action step and make sure you do it every single day. Another key strategy has been to prioritize meeting face-to-face with referral partners and making a point to build relationships.

A vital 'secret' to success is to cultivate the 'it' factor, meaning that different people have different strengths and preferences they will go to for their 'it.' This becomes important when building a team as a growth strategy.

It is important to not settle when bringing in a new team member. When interviewing candidates, keep in mind your business will benefit by having different talents onboard. Hiring the right people with the right talent, and hiring attitude over experience, are elements of their recruiting formula for success. You can teach someone how to put in an application or how to price a loan, but you can't teach someone how to have the drive to go for it. They either have that or they don't. Hiring top-notch people that they can trust to have the right attitude has allowed them to build a strong team.

Second, in terms of helping their loan officers grow their businesses, no singular sales tactic works for everybody. Identify the strength of the individual loan officer and then help them do more of it. Each of the fifteen loan officers they work with has different strengths—it's your responsibility to find that strength and encourage it if it can help them get more business. It's important to encourage it even when it's a strength that you might not have yourself.

For example, Heath and John have a loan officer whose strength is her social media game. That is not their strength but it works great for her. In fact, when that loan officer first came on board, they were a little uneasy about how she got her business. Then she proved the success it brought; the more she posted, the more volume she had, so they got behind it and encouraged her to strategically use social media. In that, Heath and John learned to be open to exploring strengths and talents beyond what they already knew, then encouraged building a team accordingly.

Another team-building tip is something that is not easy to do but is absolutely necessary, which is the ability to say no. Just like not settling in making the right hire, the ability to say no is a huge secret in plain sight. You need to say no to what doesn't work, that which doesn't prove to have a good return on your investment, to those referral partners who don't meet your specifications, to employees who are not working out, to deals or resource allocations that compromise your principles. It may be difficult in the moment but doing so will save time, energy, resources, and stress later.

Building the Future

The partnership Heath and John share has worked out remarkably well for them and their business. They complement each other. Their strengths are different and so are their weaknesses. When looking to go into a partnership, find someone different than you who will bring additional and different robust skill sets to your business. Different perspectives and points of view are needed for problem-solving and decision-making.

The strengths Heath and John have in business are because of who they are together. They do a great job of encouraging each other and playing off each other's strengths. Each sticks to what they know and does not pretend to know what they don't . . . although they know enough to cover for the other in case of vacation time. That's the beauty of their partnership—the balance and having a middle ground. There is no single person who has their combined strengths in total . . . it's just not possible. That person doesn't exist. The strengths they have in business are because of who they are together—and there is no average in that equation. They excel in different things and know when to step in or step out of a situation so excellence can consistently prevail. After eight years, they know enough about each other that there is never any point of contention between them—all it takes is a simple conversation. Their partnership now positions them and their business nicely going forward.

In terms of projecting where they will be in two years and what it will take to get there, there are big plans in motion. They just hired a very integral part of the branch as the next step for their company—an operations manager. They do not have a projection around the number of bodies on the team in two years because volume is the focus; as a production goal, they would like for Lending Path Mortgage to be doing $400 million a year in loan volume which will yield the right team mix to support it.

The operations manager is a huge part of that goal because that position will take about 80% of operational duties off Heath who can then take his talents to help implement the growth of our loan officers in a different capacity. Having an operations manager also enables John to accept even more loan officers who want to up their game. Together, these shifts will enable them to achieve the kind of growth that demonstrates their core values and principles, and paces their growth so Heath and John retain the quality of service they provide clients and staff.

Everyone's Journey Is Different

As a tangent to all that's been said, everyone's journey is different. You can never look at what the next person is doing to gauge your progress in life or business; you can only look at where you are now and where you've come from to see your growth. While you are on the path of self-growth, you have to know and accept the responsibility that it is your path and yours alone. Nobody can walk it for you. You get out of it what you put into it so you must show up for yourself. Heath and John do that as leaders; they consistently invite their loan officers and staff to do the same.

It can be good to look back and remember the people who helped you get where you are today. Even if you've outgrown them to where they are not as much help as they were a few years ago, they were part of your journey. Keep them as part of your journey moving forward even if only in your gratitude.

If given the chance to time travel back to ten years ago, changing any aspect of their experience would not bring Heath and John to where they are today. They couldn't be in a better place today than where they are right now. The journey has been remarkable; Heath and John have learned much from both the successes and the failures over a decade.

Heath and John thank the Mortgage Marketing Animals and the Freedom Club…it wasn't only their coaching and staff who helped them get where they are today—it was the people who were involved in the Club, including friends, colleagues, and even their competition. Those relationships and experiences are part of the journey. The more you learn from the people you meet, the faster you grow and the better you'll be at whatever you do.

One final thought is to always stay humble. When you are on your journey to the top, remember where you were in the beginning…you had to start somewhere. Once you get to where you think you want to be, it's important to stay humble and true to who you are—and who you were back then. It can be easy to lose sight of that and get a little cocky with success. Everyone has to start somewhere to reach success. Begin that journey with intention. Then, finally, help others where you can in their journey—it can only enrich your own.

About Heath Goodrich

Growing up in a small town in rural Wyoming, my parents taught me the value of hard work and dedication at an early age. Now, as parents of two girls of our own, my wife and I work very hard to provide for our family so we can devote time with our girls traveling, creating memories, and spending time with the rest of our family and friends. When not spending time with family and friends, you can find me on the golf course or cooking something new.

Those same principles I learned growing up and am instilling in my own children are what have guided me in building Lending Path Mortgage. Over the past eight years, my partner and I have been able to grow our company to just over 40 employees and closed over 1,200 loans with production of more than $240M annually. There have been many mentors and people over the years who have helped us get to where we are today . . . we are eternally grateful.

We guide our loan officers in achieving a strong work/life balance for themselves while increasing their personal production. We help them build a team that provides the support they need to not only grow their own business, but to give them more free time with their loved ones.

Our goal is not only to build a successful mortgage business, but to leave a legacy with our employees, partnerships, and in our communities. Personal commitment and professional excellence, coupled with a strong desire to help people are common threads with our staff and sets us apart in our market.

Heath can be reached at:

Email: **heath@lendingpathmortgage.com**

Phone: 803-361-8021

Website: **heathgoodrich.com/** | **lendingpathmortgage.com**

Facebook: **facebook.com/HeathGoodrichLendingTeam/**

LinkedIn: **linkedin.com/in/heath-goodrich-83807b19/**

About John Hinks, Jr.

Through the 33 years we have been in business, we are always looking to improve our processing and customer service. My goal is to help the client make the home buying process an enjoyable one.

My father started this company in 1983. When visiting the office as a kid, I remember the days of handwritten loan applications and sending loan packages by FedEx. But the one thing that never changed was fitting the client with the right program so that they can see success in the future.

When I am not saving the world one mortgage at a time, I love cooking BBQ and my Ron Swanson's Meat Tornado Chili that came in 2nd place at the 2012 Five Points Chili Cook off. My real passion is playing with my two children, Lucy and Jack, and helping my wife at the farm shovel horse manure and muck stalls.

And when I am not at the farm with my kids, I am a board member for the Camp Kemo Programs. I have been a counselor at Camp Kemo for 14 years and a board member for seven years. As you can see, my career feeds my family but I find it equally as important to feed my soul.

John can be reached at:

Email: **johnjr@lendingpathmortgage.com**

Phone: 803-546-0522

Website: **lendingpathmortgage.com | johnhinksjr.com/**

Facebook: **facebook.com/johnhinksjr**

LinkedIn: **linkedin.com/in/john-hinks-jr-06784815/**

Peaches, the Elevator and Self-Creation

By Scott Griffin
Founder and CEO
Scott Griffin Financial

I didn't grow up thinking mortgage banking or brokering was a good career. In fact, many of us probably don't think about it and, by fate or fortune, enter the industry through someone else's invitation, as I did. Back in 1998, I was managing apartment communities in Los Angeles and 'my' building (the one I was managing) was sold out from under me. That was my moment of choice—stay in the city but find a new career path or keep the job by transferring with the company but move out of the area.

Life tends to bring multiple growth opportunities at the same time, so naturally I was going through a stressful financial pivot as well. I needed to refinance my first purchased condo in San Diego. A beautiful woman, Peaches, lived in the apartment community I managed. We happened to get in the elevator at the same time one day, and she saw the Chase mortgage folder in my hand. I was reviewing the four or five daunting legal-sized documents inside the folder that I needed to complete. It was overwhelming. Peaches asked if I remembered she was a mortgage loan officer (I hadn't) and said she would help me. In the process of helping me successfully navigate that refinance, she suggested I would be a great person to work with her. She was just opening her own mortgage brokerage company and she was willing to train me.

My first thought was THIS was how I could stay in L.A.! I met with her because she's a positive, wonderful, generous woman. She told me all the successes available to successful mortgage brokers. The income she quoted was at levels I had never measured nor considered in my 'Befores'; not only was the potential significant but this industry invited it without restrictions. Peaches would tell me, "focus on the client's needs and your dollars will be earned" and that I would never have to worry because "there would never be a ceiling." She told me so many enticing things about why I should try it that I felt compelled. I stepped into her belief.

At the same time, I did want to be responsible and do some homework about it outside Peaches' influence. One of my apartment building employees had a dear friend in the mortgage business who was willing to have lunch with me. I wanted to hear from somebody else already in the business for objective information; I wanted to ensure Peaches wasn't being overly complimentary in trying to recruit me or build her new business.

I'll never forget that lunch. This man was very giving and very kind. He worked for a local lender, also a mortgage brokerage. He wanted me to be real about the opportunity. He asked me, "Scott, are you really willing to give up your career with your company you've been working with for over ten years? Where you are able to receive a payroll every two weeks? Where you can receive all your benefits, including retirement? You're able to be successful every day and be comfortable. Do you think giving that up in an exchange for an industry that pays only on commission is the best way for you to move forward? And why would somebody trust you with their mortgage? How long have you been doing this? And you're going to go work for a company called PeachTree what?"

As I sat with his questions, he continued. "Scott, this industry is hard to penetrate. You have to meet people and convince them they should get their 30-year mortgage with you. Probably the largest debt they'll ever adopt in life is that one. You're going to be competing with people like me who have been in the industry for many, many years. Are you sure that's something you think you should do?"

I left that lunch with those thoughts and questions rolling in my mind. I knew this man had good points. I would be competing with folks like him. I would need to learn a lot. And I would be changing careers after investing ten years in building management.

But I had learned long before then that it's impossible to fail. Failure is a mindset, not a result. Unexpected outcomes can be our greatest teachers. I knew trying something new with the idea that it's an experiment allows me to course correct. If I didn't like it, I could always go back to building management. So I took a leap of faith through Peaches' passion and joined her new brokerage.

My training consisted of going to the office in the afternoons after my day job and sitting in Peaches' office to listen as she conducted business. Then she would sit and invest time with me to educate me. Soon I was processing and becoming familiar with documents. Interestingly, my first refinance was my employee's mother's mortgage.

The Only Restrictions Are Self-Created

Once I did that first refinance, I quit my full-time career of 10+ years working in the apartment management industry to leap into this new industry of loan officer work. Obviously, I had never done it before, had only closed one client, and had nobody waiting in the pipeline for my next loan. It was a calculated risk based on those factors. However, from that decision to where I am today, I've never looked back.

That fateful and fortunate elevator ride—where I was over-whelmed as a consumer trying to refinance my own loan—with a beautiful woman who offered her help and a way for me to stay in Los Angeles by working in an industry I never knew I could fall in love with changed the rest of my life. The smallest encounter and most innocuous of events led me to, eventually, becoming the state leader for California's Lending Association.

Somehow this industry allows everything to happen—it invites everyone to win. The only restrictions on income or opportunity are the ones we self-create on our way to claiming success as a loan agent.

The Comeback

In terms of challenges, I've learned that life has different levels of understandings as we live it. While I believe it's impossible to fail, that doesn't mean everything in life works out the way we think it should because, of course, it does not. I would go so far as to say it's not supposed to because it would, eventually, get beige very quickly. Life should have surprises. Mine was a physical one in 2007. Before the mortgage industry melted down with the recession, my body shut down. I took an exit out of the industry for three years and I don't think I ever saw myself coming back. I was trying to find a dif-ferent professional path. I think many of us were trying to rediscover what life was going to be like post-recovery from 2007, 2008, 2009, and all the years after relating to the mortgage industry collapse.

The old adage is true—the bigger we are, the harder we can fall. In 2007, I was pretty big in Los Angeles. I felt like a superhero. I was in my thirties and had many levels of success I had only fantasized about as a kid. I was creating it—just like Peaches said I could. Then, all of a sudden, I didn't. And when I shut down, I shut every-thing down with the intent of not coming back.

When I did decide to make a comeback, I discovered all the tools, all the things that were so familiar in The Before, were reinterpreted through change. The same methodologies, the same relationships I had in the past, the way I approached lending . . . nothing worked the same. Everything was different.

I'm in Los Angeles where we are surrounded with jumbo loans because of the real estate price point. Jumbo lending was one of the last programs to come back after the mortgage meltdown. In 2010, when I showed up and was trying to regain my footing in the industry, it wasn't back yet. I struggled hard. It was the change of industry, oddly enough, which opened a new way for me to find solutions to my problem. My problem was I wasn't successful right NOW. I wasn't closing business for loans or creating relationships like I had in The Before. I wanted to be back in the industry successfully. I determined I needed to learn about the loan officer's compensation rule.

I searched online and found the local chapter of the California Association Mortgage Professionals—they were hosting an overview on the topic. I went that day and was in front of folks I hadn't seen for a long time, including Peaches. We stayed for a good hour or more after the meeting ended.

Through connections made there, I was soon invited to go to Congress to speak on housing reform with other fellow leaders of the Lending Association. From there, I was invited to be a leader of reform at both national and state levels as our state and national associations came together for a united front. From 2010 through 2012, I went to D.C. and got intimately involved with advocacy and reform for our industry. As a result of connections made, I met someone so powerful that the rest of my life was literally altered. I believe we meet such people at the right time when we're ready. For me, I met a coach.

Normally, I spent time in my office but I wanted to be successful. It's hard to be successful when nobody knows you're there. Accordingly, I learned first-hand the power of going to my state association meetings, of showing up, of choosing to be uncomfortable by going to the meetings and networking with people I wouldn't normally meet. That mindset allowed me to be open when speakers would present at these meetings.

The Pivot

In 2012 or 2013, Carl White presented at the state association. He shared a lot of knowledge that shifted my perspective in a big way. I heard in him that day a new path through this profession I thought I knew so well. I had never worked with a coach before; my only exposure to training was what I interpreted through Peaches and her way of doing business. And that had been a great way for me because it's how I learned how to do it. I opened my own practice in 2003 in L.A. and was successful for years through what she taught me. And yet, I didn't know what I didn't know.

At that association meeting, Carl White allowed me to hear what could happen with a plan I wasn't self-creating, sharing thoughts I had never sat with before, downloading a new view that changed everything going forward. In fact, I was sitting there the entire day listening to Carl with thoughts I had never self-created before . . . I was being flooded with insight.

In all honesty, I was pretty broke at the time. I wasn't earning much because I wasn't doing much. I was in my personal recovery process of getting back into the industry. And here was Carl White offering a three-day program in Florida in the near future. I didn't have the money for my mortgage much less coaching. I was really uncomfortable . . . but I was also very available to be different. That financial and emotional discomfort was my motivator toward taking action to get a new plan.

I didn't have cash but I had a credit card. I took that credit card and stepped into even more financial discomfort, knowing it would push me to show up differently. Everything I was learning sounded so amazing but I had a feeling I wouldn't do it on my own. I wasn't doing it before meeting Carl. If I really wanted the success I visualized having again, I bet on winning faster by doing the things that Carl and the weekend experience shared with me as tools toward success.

I took the first steps in employing the plan. I hired a virtual assistant, started team development, took advantage of what mentoring and coaching could give me. The dollars I paid to access that coaching invited me to show up in full strength. People follow their money, and so did I. Despite not being able to do it on my own before because it was uncomfortably different, I knew the discomfort was signaling growth. I kept working the plan, being uncomfortable, trying new things.

Now I'm successful in ways unlike what I could have imagined in my wildest dreams and am far beyond where I thought I'd have the right to get to in my comeback. I never dreamed I could achieve again as quickly as I did. The things I'm doing today are completely different with regard to the process, the team development strategies, the methodologies of how we approach business . . . and because of these changes, I'm on CNBC hosting a television show about real estate through the eyes of a lender. I get to have opportunities in being a state association President, going to Congress, guiding reform, creating successes I never dreamed possible—all through the art of mortgage brokering and becoming a loan agent who is willing to believe everything is possible even if it requires discomfort.

Accelerated Inspiration

My biggest takeaway from my darkest moments in this business is this: a coach can help a person move forward faster. The coachee is not alone; instead, it's about being and staying inspired. Through inspiration and guidance, the easier path is identified and actualized. That path unlocks opportunities I think many of us fantasize about and see others achieve but not might not have for ourselves—

yet. But this industry has no limits so those things are waiting for every loan officer out there.

I hope my story inspires whoever is reading it to reach out. To be crystal clear, it's my recommendation to get a professional coach but not just any coach. I'm specifically highlighting, endorsing, and recommending Carl White with the Mortgage Marketing Animals. It's their coaching program I personally tested, activated, employed, and am currently in love with as it has afforded the successes my family enjoys right now. Their passion to share guidance with those of us who can connect with them fuels transformation on multiple levels.

I met Carl when it was literally my darkest point and he was my bright light. As a result of his coaching, I'm sitting here in Big Bear with three houses. I actually own five. I have nine full-time staff members. I have nothing pulling at my shoulders. The reason for that is because I'm so bless-fully successful . . . I'm on TV now . . . I have great clients . . . all of it is like fantasy stuff but it's all real. And it's because I started doing things that were uncomfortable. It's because I started doing things that I believed I had the right to try. I understood that the 'new' would be available inside of the uncomfortable when I was willing to step out and experiment. Change itself would invite a different experience and fresh results. So I just kept doing it. And I still keep doing it.

Having It Together

There are a couple of tips I would offer to help loan officers. First, don't do it alone. It helps for you and I to get more opportunities when we're not trying to wear all the hats all the same time. Through team development, we're able to transfer some of our multiple hats to the other people we bring on to the team we create and develop. By transferring hats to others, we loan officers are able to do more together.

I've learned it's the 'more together' which allows us to build large pipelines that close successfully and consistently. We're not trying to fish or hunt for the loan, then bring the loan home, clean the loan, then cook the loan, then serve the loan. Instead, we share that responsibility with others on our team. But we can only do that by stepping into the discomfort of team development, to delegate and trust team members to do it right, to pay for team members for their work. Personally, I had to readjust my thought process to get comfortable paying for team members versus me doing it alone. Here's how I did it.

The simple truth is I adjusted my thoughts. I realized payroll wasn't an expense as much as an investment. I wasn't available for making more expenses but I'm often open-minded to invest. When investing, it's like standing in front of that magical machine where you put $2 in and you get $10 back. However, the machine doesn't pay out unless we put something in first. Shifting from an expense mindset to an investment mindset is a game-changer for any business owner.

That said, it will stretch you to build a team, especially at first. The good news is today's technology enables team building in new ways. The world has gotten much closer through the internet. Telephones are no longer tethered to a cord. You can actually find talent in other countries. My first team member hire was someone from the Philippines where my dollar, given currency conversion, goes farther than it does here in America. That allowed me to afford my first team member. Don't do it alone—find a way to get help.

As for my second tip, here's the magic secret: self-thought is valuable. Thoughts are things. I often walk early in the morning for two to three hours. I sit and reflect and appreciate things in life because I'm often so busy I rarely preserve time to reflect later in the day. Reflection gets you out of the urgent into the important. In reflecting life, you consider and feel gratitude for things—the invitations, the relationships, the circumstances and more—that showed up for you.

You can shape your mindset through intentional morning thoughts. For me, that mindset gets activated through physical movement. When I'm moving, there is a flow of oxygen and blood and energy. Feel-good endorphins are stimulated; my mind starts building thoughts that play out during the day.

Positive thoughts invite positive things and, conversely, the same is true of negative thoughts. Those morning walks are priceless for me in finding and tuning into the spirit of positivity and light that I can tune in and bring through for most of my day. Not every day is as easy as others and, again, they're not supposed to be . . . those challenges help you grow, become resilient, and show you where you have as-yet-unrecognized strength. Those challenges give you a reason to take another walk, to reflect again, to start over. The next day's self-thought allows everything else to play out that next day, and the day after. Work on your self-thought and know everything is possible.

Just as the fruit of a tree does not show the root system, or a skyscraper does not show the sub-floors, success is not only what is visible. The combination of having a plan, working the system, cultivating clean self-thought for conscious creation, and taking consistent uncomfortable action are what most people will never see; instead, people see only the outcomes of that focus. You have to know the value of that kind of personal infrastructure. You have to put your investment in to get a sizeable return back.

Self-Beliefs Create Conscious (and Unconscious) Results

In terms of closing the most loans in my career, I have to give credit to team development as a key strategy. Your team can help you create the biggest successes because you do what only you can do while they do what they do. My secret to effective team building, which will be no surprise by now, is self-belief. Self-belief empowers building a team by doing what it takes . . . to get up extra early, to take that morning walk, to reflect in the face of a daunting daily schedule, to write a payroll check even when there are not yet new loans to support the payroll check. When you do the work, the law of cause and effect takes over—there is no other outcome except business growth when you have self-belief, the right team, and a good system in place.

Not to be a broken record about what has worked well for me, but if there was just one thing I would do again to grow my business, it would be to hire a great coach much sooner. The number one thing that helped me do things I was not doing in 'The Before' is I had to have thoughts I wasn't self-creating. I had to go beyond what I knew. When left alone, like every other human on the planet, I did whatever I thought I should be doing based on what I already knew. Clearly, that was not getting me the results I wanted and needed in my business. That was a self-imposed limitation.

By getting the right coach, I was given new thoughts to think, new ideas to examine, new perspectives to play out, new strategies to test and new experiments to put in motion. I simply had to put into practice that which I was learning.

Today, I am known for being an implementer. Why is it I can implement even when it pushes the edges of my comfort zone? It's because I'm a believer. I can implement effectively because I consistently go on those morning walks to reflect and remind myself that, even when it looked like I couldn't in the past, I did. When you do enough of those 'impossibles' in life, you get bold. You get to where you believe you can because you saw the impossible become possible because you did it. You discover your own capabilities. You see the strength you didn't know you had . . . and you see that what was calling you was meant for you. All you had to do was everything to be aligned with it. (Read that one twice.) When you can reflect on enough of those stories, you cannot help but be bolder, stronger, and more inspired tomorrow.

Fantasize The Future

I often fantasize about where I see myself in two years and what will get me there. As a result, I have found it's wickedly important to keep 'want' activated. I believe activating 'want' is either the instigation or the inspiration to do things because desire invites new activities and accomplishments. Without want, what pulls you forward? Unless you have a want, there is no reason to change. Nothing will be different, at least intentionally, without wanting something new.

So I want to live by the water—the ocean or the beach. I'd also love to have a larger, bolder company brand with an expanded footprint in the market. While there's nine of us now, I would love to develop our team to a much bigger number as a result of expanding our footprint. I would love more television time; I hope this series I'm a part of now continues to be successful and expands my ability to find a presence through media. I expect to increase my media footprint through not only television but through publishing a magazine, using social networks, hiring an associate producer, and continuing to do things differently. I'm not going to get what I want if I don't do things I wasn't doing before. In other words, to get what I want means doing new things; otherwise, I will keep getting the same old results. I'll continue to take action in the spirit of 'I believe I can.' I will step into being uncomfortable, take on new experiments, cultivate my self-belief, and have fun along the way. Given my results over the last two years, the next two years could take me to places I cannot even imagine yet.

So who will you meet on an elevator today? What thoughts are you self-creating? What do you really want? And how willing are you to be uncomfortable to have it? This is your moment of choice. Go for it.

About Scott Griffin

I began my career in 1986 as a residential property specialist. My focus was on leasing and managing large luxury apartment communities for real estate investment management firms, such as Kennedy Wilson, Heitman and JMB Properties.

After that, I moved on to become a mortgage loan agent, and was quickly promoted to branch management of Peachtree Financial. These experiences helped shape my understanding of the real estate and mortgage industries (and also helped open my eyes to their vast opportunities)!

In 2003, I opened my namesake mortgage brokerage in Los Angeles, later expanding to offices in San Diego and Palm Springs.

Currently, Scott Griffin Financial specializes in A' Paper Jumbo Loans for clients who are self-employed or in the entertainment industry. I'm proud to say that our work has funded more than $831 million in purchase and refinance home loans over just the past eight years!

I've been a champion for homeowners' rights and mortgage industry reform for a long time. As the 2016-2017 President of the California Association of Mortgage Professionals, I've made it my daily work to engage with industry leaders, regulatory bodies, and homebuyers alike.

My work as president of the association earned me the prestigious 2016 Broker of the Year Award, an honor I gratefully accepted.

I've traveled as close as Sacramento and as far as Washington, D.C. to speak to members of Congress and the Senate on housing reform. My advocacy, influence, and passion have helped transform many key reforms in the mortgage industry into law.

This work has gotten me and my team recognized by U.S. Congressman Gary Miller, California State Senator Mike Morrell, and California State Congressman Bill Dodd — all of whom work to support this thriving industry.

I truly love helping property owners connect with the right funding at the right time to make their ownership dreams come true.

Scott can be reached at:

Email: **scott@scottgriffin.com**

Phone: 310-456-4494

Website: **ScottGriffin.com**

Facebook: **facebook.com/scottgriffinfinancial/**

LinkedIn: **linkedin.com/in/scottgriffinfinancial/**

Faith, Fun and Finance

By Chris Haynes
Branch Manager and Loan Officer
Peoples Home Equity

Dumb luck was the catalyst for my career as a loan officer. Back in 2003, I was in college with no real idea of what I wanted to do. My sister's then-boyfriend, a loan officer, introduced me to the industry as a career option. He said I could do well and even run my own business, which seemed like a good idea. I said, "That sounds like a good career, seems fun, and something I would potentially enjoy doing." It was dumb luck to even hear about the mortgage business much less have a way to get into it. I fell my way into success. And feel very blessed and fortunate to have had God intervene on my behalf.

I think my biggest challenge, out of many in the mortgage business, was learning how to grow. Everybody wants to do more loans and help more people, but how do you do that? This inherently led to my next challenge. I had to have a team of great people around me to help with the business. One person has only 40 to maybe 60 or even 70 hours a week, if you want to work that much... at some point, you just physically run out of time. So the biggest challenge in everybody's business is how to help more people and get more done in the same amount of time (or less), then learning how to cultivate a team and create a great environment for a team to thrive.

When I got into the business, I was the guy who would go to all the sales seminars. Brian Tracy is a sales guru who has been around for a while. He came to Nashville around 2005 or 2006 and did a sales presentation. I thought it was great. I went to the back of the room and bought the whole $300 deal, all twenty CDs on time management and sales and all that stuff. I listened to them. I took notes. I absorbed it. I just wanted to be really good at what I did. I also went to some Tony Robbins events. Any loan officers who are looking for a good seminar, Tony Robbins is not really into mortgage coaching and he doesn't coach directly on mortgages, but I really love Tony Robbins and his work.

Back in 2008, I opened my own branch and was growing my business—I was doing ok. It was a lot of fun and very small because I was the branch manager and my brother was a loan officer with me. He did a great job both then and now. That was also the year the market crashed. The next three years were full of challenges.

In 2011, I decided to get coaching around business development. I joined a well-known coaching company and it definitely changed how I was doing things. Coaching taught me systems to grow the business as well as how to hire great people to help me close the business. It's not good enough to just bring business in—you have to be able to lock it down and deliver on it. It takes a lot of work and physical hours to do a good job to get a deal closed for your clients. Having the right systems and a team in place to streamline the process is critical to business development. And I got it together by working with a coach and mentor.

Follow Experience

Finding people who are further down the same road I am on who have experience, getting their advice, learning from them, and doing what they do to get to positive results quicker is the number one thing I did to contribute to my own success. After my first full year of coaching, I tripled my business. By that I do not mean production, because I didn't know exactly what that was, but income— I tripled my income. From there I kept working the system and growing my business.

During this time, I was working too many hours and pretty stressed out. It was great to have the income but I still needed to figure out how to turn my job into a business. I wanted to be home with my kids when they had stuff going on, to be able to take time off with my wife when I wanted, to take my foot off the gas without it affecting my income. I needed to enjoy the life I was working so hard to build. It doesn't really matter how much money you make if you don't enjoy it. If you don't have freedom to do the things you want to do, life's not fun. Who cares how much money you have in life, if it's not fun?

I heard about Carl White and his teachings on freedom. So I decided to switch coaching to The Freedom Club so I could figure out how to structure my business to where I had some freedom while still being able to do lots of loans and close lots of business.

If I had to do it all over again, I would tell myself to think and dream bigger. I know now that you can do more than you think you can. Thinking bigger goes hand in hand with not being afraid to hire the next team member faster. Growing your team faster is what, ultimately, gives you the ability to produce more. So I would get a great mentor and run with what you learn, think bigger, know you can do more, and hire faster.

Start Where You Are and Use Systems

While I've advised what a great mentor can do to help you, it's important to clarify that person could be a coach you hire, somebody in your office who can help you when you're on that road, or maybe a branch manager who will teach you what you need to know. If there's not a branch manager, maybe another experienced loan officer in the business...they might even be from another company. The point is to find somebody who is experienced and who you can learn from in a real-world scenario. You need to start where you are with someone who has been there and grown from it too.

If you're doing one loan a month or three, and you want to learn how to do ten loans a month, talk to somebody who's doing 10 or 20 loans a month so they can teach you the right systems. You'll reduce your learning curve and compress time vs. figuring out and recreating the systems on your own.

Systems are really the key to handling routine and repetitive tasks. When you know the day-to-day stuff is handled, you have time to think bigger, be more strategic, make changes in other areas to increase your outcomes, and more.

I used to have a really sophisticated lead tracking system. I called it "sticky notes." That's a joke by the way, but it's a horrible lead tracking system. You get a new lead, it goes on a sticky note, you lose the sticky note after two days, and you never call them back. So I started using a lead tracking system I got from my coaching program.

Putting those systems in place is a repeatable process. You want your business to metaphorically be like McDonald's: everybody comes in and gets the same experience. I don't necessarily want my business compared to McDonald's, but I want it to run with that kind of efficiency. When the customers come in and get the same predictably great service, the systems make sure their expectations are met, the systems ensure we have what we need to do a great job.

Having good systems and structure means you can train your team members on how you want to do things. Everything can be a system—tracking all your leads, tracking activities, monitoring loan milestones so the same things happen every time—to ensure you're not just running your business haphazardly. You need to know that, when a new borrower comes in, the exact same steps happen every time whether it's you or your team member talking to your client. Your mentor probably has a lot of that in place and can help you put that in place for your own business.

Work Your Database

The one strategy that has resulted in the most closed loans for me is probably tracking and working my database over the long-term. Of course, I work with business partners and realtors and the 'standard' industry relationship-building strategies to consistently expand my circle. But the biggest mistake I see most young loan officers make is they don't have, and are not working or building, a database. I don't know where I picked it up but, in my first year in the business, I started keeping up with everybody's name I worked with in closed loans. I didn't know it then but I was building a database in an Excel spreadsheet. In fact, I didn't work it great. I didn't have systems or technology around working the spreadsheet / database but I did keep up with my people. I managed to mail them a couple of times a year and I stayed in touch.

Over the years, I built my database of closed business and pre-approved clients. It's probably around 2,000 people at this point. We have a very structured system we use to stay in touch with them. We mail them old-fashioned, tangible snail mail in the form of handwritten envelopes or postcards once a month. We also email them once a week. We have four to five client appreciation events per year. We call or text them on their birthday, and we send a birthday card too. We pay attention to what's happening in their lives and acknowledge the milestones—weddings, anniversaries, new babies, etc. Then we take great care of their loans and make referrals on services and act as a community resource for them.

Simply working with my database and keeping up with all those people is the number one thing that's helped me close business that a lot of loan officers miss. Now you can build relationships with business partners, builders, and realtors, and that has closed lots and lots of business for me too—that's how I started to build the database. But if there's one strategy I can tell somebody to do, it would be to build that database and then work it consistently. Showing up consistently is a differentiator. When you do it, you'll be able to keep up with your clients to help them over and over and get referrals from them over time.

Appreciate Clients

I love doing client appreciation events. We've hosted movie nights at our local theater and had an ice cream social. We hired the ice cream truck to come to our office. We've hosted Thanksgiving lunch and pictures with Santa. Our intention is to appreciate our clients and offer connections in practical ways that make sense.

The Secret Sauce

Hands down, hiring people to help you on your journey is one of the best things you can do for your business. One secret to building my team has been hiring fun, great people—the right kind of people who know the mortgage business and have the skills. The right person makes all the difference. Second, once you find the right person, you need to make sure you have a great place for them to work. If they're not the right person, the environment is not going to matter. But when they are, the environment is what allows them to give their best.

We want our office to have a family atmosphere. Personally, I am a Christian and I run my business through my faith. I try to treat everybody the way I want to be treated. I want my office to be a safe place for people to come and work. Staff is never going to get cursed at, yelled at, marginalized, or disrespected. That includes even if they have a different opinion because they might see something that would otherwise get missed. If not, that's simply an opportunity to do some training.

Now, I have to say we have really high expectations. We expect people to work hard and do a great job. We expect them to take great care of our clients. But we make the work environment a place people want to be. I want it to be a home away from home. Everybody has their home and that's where they're going to be the most comfortable. Home is where they're going to have their family. However, we want the office to be just as comfortable in being a great place to work.

When people are comfortable, they're going to do a great job for and with your clients. You're going to have longevity with employees who want to stay with you and your company long-term. Turnover, recruiting, and replacing employees is very costly and time-consuming—it sets you back every time. So when you find those right people, treat them right so you keep them.

In fact, it is my team that has allowed me to have a greater life balance. In addition to my loan business, I also had a stint as a mortgage coach. I greatly loved and enjoyed it. Eventually, I stepped back from coaching because I wanted more time and more freedom with my family. But paying it forward is both humbling and a way to share the benefit of what you've learned over a lifetime.

In terms of business, having a mentor or coach is the number one thing loan officers need because our businesses and our lives are pretty much crazy. I talk to loan officers in different companies all the time. Most of them work a lot of hours and don't have much control over their personal time. Some of them have personal lives that aren't much fun. Working with a coach who can help you get those systems in place and hold you accountable to your commitments can be a game-changer.

Outside the Known Zone

My faith helps me believe that life is happening for me, not to me. Everything works out for me—even things that are setbacks in the short-term work out in the long run. In 2008, the market crash was an exceedingly hard time to be in the business. Folks who stuck it out three, four or five years later, we're doing much, much, much, much better. In fact, I would say we are typically doing two or three times better than what we were doing prior to 2008.

When you allow mistakes to happen and learn from them, you allow yourself to grow, and grow, and grow. When you make the wrong decision or feel like you made the wrong decision, things are always working out for you. You simply have to look for the silver lining, find it, be open to learning from it, and always keep growing.

Personally, I have had to grow to help my business grow. Your business can only grow as fast as you do. One of the ways I've had to grow is getting comfortable with public speaking and visibility. I'm not naturally a public speaker. I don't seek public attention. But through growing my business and in trying to help more people, I've become comfortable with getting up and talking to groups, both small and even fairly large now. In fact, I've talked to a few hundred people in a room at a time. That's definitely something 10–15 years ago I did not want to do and had no inkling of a desire to do. Like most people, I was scared to get up and speak in front of people. They say the fear of public speaking is greater than the fear of dying. I'm not sure I could say it went that far for me but becoming comfortable with speaking in front of people is definitely something that made me step outside my comfort zone and grow as a business professional and leader.

I was also not a big fan of growing a team. That was not something I wanted to do. I had to step outside my comfort zone to hire my very first team member because I didn't want to hire a team member. I just wanted to do more business and then realized I didn't have enough hours in the week to make all that happen. So your business pushes you to grow personally to grow your business results. It's just part of the process.

Do Good While Doing Well

I've been growing my business, hiring, and coaching more loan officers, and I really enjoy that. Running my own branch as a business allows me to have freedom. Coaching other loan officers who want to learn what I've done and how I've done it to shortcut their way to success is rewarding. I believe I can teach a loan officer how to be extraordinarily successful in a short period of time, much shorter than it took me. It took me probably eight years to go from zero to doing really good business and making good money. I believe I can take a loan officer who's been in business for a year or two and, in two or three years, get him or her to that same level if they have the desire and ability to follow directions.

My desire is to have more loan officers that I can coach to do the same things I do to be successful. The goal is to just continue loving life and spending time with my family. Doing good while doing well for others.

In 2016, my team and I did 355 units. It was during that time when I hit a breaking point, honestly. I was stressed out. It was too much work. I wasn't home every night to see my kids like I wanted to be . . . it wasn't what I wanted my business to look like on a day-to-day basis. So with Carl's help, I started concentrating on my team, building up who was already there and getting the right new team members in place. I'm still working on that.

But in 2019, I had my best year ever AND I was out of the office for eleven—yes 11!—different weeks. I could have never done that just a few years before.

This year we will close about 700 units and I'm working approximately 35 hours a week. I coach my loan officers. I coach my team. My stress level went from a nine (in 2016) to a two or three even while doubling my loan closures. I'm still in the mortgage business so my stress levels are above zero. But the reduction in stress is a testament to working with my mentors, the coaches I've had, and the mindset shift in me. As a loan officer, you have to have the mindset shift. You can't just take on what your coaches say—you have to decide that it's what you want and then work to do it. Then you can make it happen.

Design Your Life First

I coach my loan officers to know this: design your life first. What time do you want to be home? If you've got kids' softball, baseball, basketball, whatever games on the weekends, put that in your calendar and put it into your calendar first. In this business, you can work 80 hours a week. I've known people who have worked 100 hours a week. If that's what you love to do, that's fine. But that is not more important than your health or your family. Money is not more important than my family.

Now sometimes people say that but their actions don't align because they're so busy and they don't want to let anybody down. "I have got to call this person back." "I need to get this thing done." "I have got to stay at work until eight o'clock tonight and I'm sorry."

You do that over and over, and your life passes you by. So try to set those boundaries upfront. Know your trade-offs. If your business grows a little slower than it would have if you were working 70 hours a week, maybe you can be okay with that. Set your parameters and take care of your family first. Your business will still thrive. Mine did.

It also helps you to learn to hire and delegate (and do it faster) when you aren't willing to just get busier and work an extra 20 or 30 hours every week to get it done. You know you're going to hire to get it done through a great team.

One last note . . . I would add in here a plug for Carl and his coaching company. If you don't have a coach, hire him. Just do it. Carl did not ask me to say that. If you're looking to grow your mortgage business and have more freedom in your life, you should hire a coach and Carl and his company are great. There are other great companies out there too—whatever flavor you like is fine. But I would definitely recommend you hire a coach. If you're open to talking to the Mortgage Marketing Animals, you can't go wrong with them—they have proven systems and they really care about your success.

In 2016, Carl did a presentation for my company. I connected with him on a personal level and have been talking directly to Carl ever since, for nearly four years now. At the time we met, I was burnt out. I needed to shift my business to where I had more time with my family. And Carl was a huge help in that. I saw how he ran his business and what he did and how he did it. It's kind of funny . . . most people don't believe it's possible. If I tell people what I do, like, "Hey, I'm closing 700 loans this year and I'll work 35 hours a week. I've taken quite a bit of vacation," they aren't sure they could believe that's true. I did not *not* believe it. But I knew Carl did it. I just didn't believe I could do it. It was one of those things where I knew what Carl was doing and I didn't doubt he could do it. I'm just saying I didn't know that I could do it. I'm not on Carl's level—Carl was on a completely different level.

But here's what I know now . . . if you design it right, and you have a plan of where you want to be, and you know how important it is to have freedom and not just make money, then you can absolutely make your best life happen through your business.

About Chris Haynes

Whether it's shooting three-pointers, fishing with his three sons or helping a new borrower structure a loan in a way that fulfills their dream of home ownership, Chris Haynes is going to work hard to be sure his efforts are successful.

Born in Kentucky, Chris now calls Mt. Juliet, TN, home with his wife, Melissa and three boys, Brayden, Jackson, and Jordan. He loves hunting and fishing with his boys and being an active part of his church family at Mt. Juliet Church of Christ.

Chris feels very blessed to have started his career at Peoples Home Equity in 2004. He believes Peoples Home Equity has given him the ability to learn the mortgage business and now run his business and serve his clients and community in his own way. He has led the branch in Mt. Juliet for more than ten years.

Being part of a nationwide company gives Chris the ability to give his clients the best financial products available today. Because he believes in the importance of relationships, Chris and his team take the time to try and meet every client and every realtor in person to ensure they are taking care of their mortgage needs.

Chris and his brother, Clint, started the branch in 2008 with just the two of them. They have now successfully grown to a branch of more than twenty employees and serve hundreds of clients each year.

And yes, Chris still holds the record at his alma mater, Freed Hardiman University, for most three-point shots in a single basketball game—just in case you wondered.

Chris Hanes | Branch Manager / Mortgage Adviser
NMLS #170397
Chris can be reached:

Email: **chaynes@peopleshomeequity.com**

Phone: 615-945-3994

Website: **phelending.com**

LinkedIn: **linkedin.com/in/chris-haynes-66893211/**

Generous People Generate

By Brett Lindquist
CEO
The Mortgage Firm

Fate made me a loan officer. Growing up, I never lived in a house until I was 13. We moved a lot. My father worked for the Sheraton hotels so I lived in hotels all over the country—we moved 17 or 18 times by the time I turned twenty. What's funny is that I went to Florida State University and, when I signed up for a major, I signed up for hotel restaurant management. Later, I thought, 'what the heck am I doing?' I watched my father work all the time as a 24/7 resident manager. So soon as I arrived on campus at Florida State, I changed my major and ended up graduating with two degrees—one in finance and the other in real estate. I also swam on the swim team and was team captain my senior year. Yes, I'm an overachiever. :)

After college, I came home from school to stay with my parents and interview for jobs. Someone connected me with a mortgage broker because of my degrees—and I was off to the races with my first job interview!

A quick side note: I remember at 13 years old standing in front of my parent's newly purchased first home and thinking, "How do people do this? How do they buy homes like this?" In retrospect, it is a strange coincidence that I had that particular thought, which became a thread through my education, which then carried me into the mortgage business professionally. I think we always have the answers we need when we stop and pay attention.

During that first interview with the mortgage broker, the guy blew me away. In fact, he freaked me out. He said, "You're going to make a hundred grand. You're going to get a new car. You're going to have an expense account. You're going to get new tires on your car every six months." As a 23-year old, I was bouncing with dreams and excitement! When I got up to leave that interview, I couldn't even find my way out of his office. There were a couple of turns and I was flying high. Funny thing is I never heard from him again. The guy never returned my phone calls. But I was intrigued about the business.

Shortly after that, I connected with someone I knew in Orlando who was a mortgage banker—an awesome guy named Doug Turner. Luck was, once again, intervening on my behalf. He helped me get my start in the business when I went to work for him. He assembled a really great group of people, both loan officers and staff. We had a lot of fun. I soaked in everything I could learn because I was new to the business. This has served me incredibly well over the span of my career.

Just Keep Moving

As I got further into the business, one of the biggest challenges I needed to overcome was burnout. I think because I had moved so much in my youth, I felt like I needed to keep moving. Throughout my twenties, every three or four years, I'd call my folks and say, "I just...I can't. I don't want to do this anymore. I can't stand it. And I want to move." My mother would say, "Well, where can you make that much money?" I'd say, "Money isn't everything." Then I'd go back and get into it again. That cyclical burnout was somewhat predictable; the only way I knew to recover from it was to just keep diving back into the business. I kept moving by focusing on what was coming next vs. making a physical move. It was a mindset shift that allowed me to do whatever came next.

Being a loan officer requires having a really good work ethic. Our business is all about developing relationships, which I enjoy— I really like meeting people from different cities and states. Given my history with moving around so much, I had grown up hearing different dialects and accents. As a result, when I'd speak with someone, I would guess where they were from and, a lot of times, I was right. In that way, moving a lot was helpful because I could create instant rapport with people I had just met.

Another challenge I encountered was developing a really good business plan and sticking to it. Today there are great coaching resources, like the Marketing Animals, that give you structure. But back in the eighties, there were only coaching tapes, CDs, and maybe live events—but it wasn't like it is now where you can get a comprehensive game plan. Then, and now, the key to success is developing your plan and sticking with it. How did I overcome that hurdle given my propensity to keep moving? I just worked my plan. I went against that urge to give up, to move, to do something different—I just stuck with it.

Still another challenge that wasn't so apparent when I started, and is still an issue today, was the disadvantage of being young. When I got into the business, I was 23 years old. I would work with realtors whose average age was in their forties or fifties, looking at this 20-something year old loan officer. They would be thinking, 'there's no way this newbie knows that much about this business.' As a lender, you're holding the realtor's commission in your hands until it closes. So one of the biggest obstacles when I was younger was realtors who would not refer me business because I was young and single. In their worldview, I wasn't as stable as someone with a family to support.

The odds are against you when you're a younger loan officer. You have a huge learning curve, you don't have relationships built yet, and you're new to negotiations and objection handling. As a result, you must have an even better work ethic than anyone else. You really have to know the business. You have to stay on top of being in touch with your referral partners and clients. And you absolutely have to give unparalleled service. Whether that's returning calls quickly, making extra calls in a day, or getting your hustle on, you—as a younger person in this business—simply have to work harder than when you're older with more business experience and connections.

In my case, by sticking to my plan, knowing it was going to work even if there were ups and downs and tough times, and giving great service, the results have been extremely good. Yes, there are tough times. There are also good times. When you know your plan works, you just have to apply it again over and over. Listen to your inner wisdom. Success means feeling good about recharging your business with a plan you can rely on to work for results.

Reach Higher

If I could go back in time to talk to myself ten years ago, I would tell myself to believe what I saw the future to be—and then reach higher. For me, it's about being not only a goal-setter but a big goal-setter to really push my achievement potential. Experts will tell you to not set goals too high because if / when you can't achieve them, you'll lose momentum. However, in my mind, a big goal is just a bigger reach. Stretch to reach higher than what you think you can do as long as you're willing to put the work in and give spectacular customer service. You have to put more in to get more.

If I could give a loan officer any word of advice it would be this: first set big-huge goals, then have a well-defined plan, which is tied into having a coach or a mentor. It's definitely important to get a coach, particularly a mortgage coach, who really knows what they're doing because the accountability with them is what can push you to your next level. There will be times you don't want to do something, even though you know it's the right next thing(s) to do. So even if you don't want to do those things, you'll feel like you have to follow through and do them because your coach wants and expects you to do it. Even more, you paid them to tell you what to do so to not do it is a disservice to your own investment.

I would also say plan on working smarter than your competition. How do you do that? Simply look at what very small part of your daily activity actually brings in the leads for your mortgage business, and then spend more time doing that and less time doing anything else. When you do that and get your systems and strategies in place, and you've developed the relationships you need for generating business, you can dial back on the hours even more and work even less. However, it is ideal to front-end load your success. Relationship development and delivering spectacular service underlie everything else you do in business.

Because of my swimming career from age five to twenty-two, I've had many coaches throughout my life, usually three to five at a time. Even now, I have a trainer / workout coach, a recruiting coach to help me grow my team, a mortgage coach who helps with business strategy and systems, and a spiritual/life coach who helps integrate life beyond work. I'm a big fan of having at least one coach, primarily because of the accountability. You'll accomplish more when you have a coach because they have a different perspective and access to knowledge beyond what you already know. They can guide you, or push you if needed, to where you'll accomplish more than you ever thought possible.

One of the activities that gives me great joy and allows me to give back is sitting on the board of the business school at Florida State University. I'm also on the board of the Boosters for sports. Through the business school, I mentor students every year on different business practices and ideas, helping them learn by sharing real-world knowledge. The reality is I probably get more out of it than they do because it's really great helping a young person get started. What's super cool is when the students share some of the things the mentor (like me) taught them. It's incredible to hear the things they repeat back that were shared with them and which they took in . . . these insights and connections are going to help them throughout their life and business career.

Connection, Connection, Connection

The one strategy that has closed the most loans for me is developing as many realtor relationships as possible. There are different strategies on how to do that though. One way is to cold call realtors out of a magazine or directory. You can ask friends, family, and business acquaintances about realtors they know which makes it more of a warm connection. A significant strategy to use is going after the listing agent on a current transaction; in fact, that's the best way because they can watch you perform during that process and likely will feel comfortable sending you referrals after that transaction closes. The bottom line is it's vital to develop the most relationships you can through service, authenticity, and helping people get what they want—period.

When I coach the Florida State kids (and anybody who asks), I always recommend casting a wide net. I have a group of about twenty business owners who I'm involved with from when I was in a CEO group. I've also been involved with my local Chamber of Commerce so there's a bunch of people with which to build relationships. Then connecting within our industry is another group of people. When you live your life and show up, you will naturally meet people. Casting a wide net is the overall strategy but, within that, the realtors sell homes so they are, naturally, a primary category for focus. Once you meet all these people, keep showing up, offer value where you can, and deliver on what you promise.

Another connection that I would say is the secret to success is hiring the right person. Back in the day, we didn't have the personality or skill assessments that are available today. Those make it a little easier to tell who someone is now ... but, back then, you had to interview people and use your judgment. We still interview, obviously, but now we have the benefit of additional resources to help make a quality decision.

The way we've grown our team, and really our company, is by personal referrals. If someone knows a person who is looking for a new professional home and who has a great work ethic, is stellar with people, or comes with high integrity and good character, that is the best way to make a long-lasting hire. Currently, we have 50 branches and almost all of them are staffed with friends of friends or from referrals from current team members, business contacts like a title company referral or a credit bureau and other business partners. That referral is a good starting point for our recruitment process.

In terms of our corporate culture, one thing that's nice for people who join us is we run our business like a family business. We're all about relationships. You can ask any of our branch managers about how we work; each will confirm I have a personal relationship with them—a good one. It's not fluff or show. I sincerely enjoy talking with our managers and producers.

Back to the Future

When the mortgage meltdown hit in 2008 / 2009, we only had one branch and business got really bad. We had to do something different. By the way, when I say 'we,' I'm one of three partners in the company—we're still together after 25 years. The chances of three guys staying together in the same business for 25 years is like one in 60 million or some ridiculous number. It's unheard of for three partners stay together for that long. It's cool to look at how well our relationships have served each other and our company.

Anyway, back in 2008, we decided we just had to do something or our business would fail. So we decided to open new branches. We recruited our first few branches in Tampa, Lakeland, and Jupiter, FL; expanding our branches is how we have continued to grow. It was counterintuitive to take that kind of risk because I would say maybe 80% of mortgage businesses failed back then. But we were one of the few still standing so we just decided to grow in the face of complete adversity. It's worked out really well for us in the long run.

We always base our growth and hiring decisions on who we want to work with that we think is a good fit for our values. It starts with do we like the person and do they have good character. Also, one of our brand strategies when adding an existing branch to our company portfolio is that we allow them to maintain their name for local brand recognition, powered by The Mortgage Firm. That community-building approach honors existing relationships and makes a smoother transition.

We will continue to grow with new team members and new branches. We're also excited about some future trends and projections. I believe millennials are a huge target market who will continue buying homes. We focus on the purchase business as people will always buy homes. We stay in front of our referral partners. Rates may fluctuate but focusing on the purchase business ensures success. Focusing solely on the currently lucrative refi refinance business without connecting with your referral sources is a recipe to be forgotten. It is a case of 'out of sight, out of mind.'

With that said, when we do loans for any of our clients, we help them with refinancing too. It's our responsibility to help our clients save money. If there's a better product or a better payment plan for them, our duty is to help them know that. Our philosophy is that our clients are lifelong relationships. We want to help them buy their next house. We want to help their kids buy their homes. We want to help their family members and their referrals. We have consistently focused on developing those deep relationships with our clients.

Another projection that will impact our business is something I found interesting in a book by Harry S. Dent, Jr. called *The Roaring 2000s*, written in 1989. In that book, Harry forecasted the economy and the stock market for the next several decades. He projected the Dow would be at 10,000 by the year 2000, that is exactly what happened. He also forecasted that the Japanese economy would crash and that happened. He calculated based on birth rates. He also forecasted we would have a recession/depression in 2009. So twenty years prior to the mortgage meltdown, Harry forecasted our economy would tank. A lot of people think it was the mortgage meltdown that led our economy to tank but the reality is our economies are based on birth rates. Let me explain.

The baby boomer generation is from people who came back from war and had just a ton of kids. There was a huge amount of people moving through that time period. As a result, starting in the late eighties through the 2000's, baby boomers were buying houses, cars, boats, toilet paper, cereal, and all the stuff that goes with having a massive population. Following that surge in population growth, we had a dip in birth rates, which is what caused the economic drop.

Harry S. Dent, Jr. also wrote that the economy would tank in 2009 because the baby boomers would be aging and would sell their big home to buy a smaller one or get out of the market altogether. As a result, real estate would tank and, he said, they would sell all their stocks and buy bonds, which are a lot more secure. Naturally, this would tank the stocks, which is exactly what happened in 2008/2009-ish. Now the millennials are the next huge mass of people. Because of millennials, the future looks great. They live with their parents longer. They wait longer to get married. They're waiting to have babies longer, but they're in full force right now. In fact, 40% of our market are millennials but that number will increase from here.

Additionally, older people are not necessarily downsizing like they were which may be due to longer lifespans or holding on to wealth or some other reason. The point is they're still in the real estate market. From everything I'm hearing and understanding, it sounds like we should have a really good market for the next six to ten years.

Manageable Growth

In terms of our company's future vision, we've always wanted, and have achieved, manageable growth. It's not worth growing just to grow. You have to maintain excellent service and TAKE CARE OF YOUR EMPLOYEES! If you are growing and everyone is so busy that they are not enjoying what they are doing, it's not worth it. We are always focused on making sure we have enough support staff for growth. Whether you have an origination team or a company, having the right amount of support members is the key.

We also focus on bridging the gap between sales and support. Salespeople might tend to appear more pushy or aggressive than other people but that is just their personality style. They don't intend to be mean but they can really upset operations-oriented people without realizing it. Support people can tend to be more analytical, on the quiet side, and be more calculated. They need to think about things before just jumping into action, which can be a trigger for salespeople who are all about the now, now, NOW. It's important for salespeople, who are driven to get results, to speak to support people, who are driven to cover the details, in a way that elicits their help, meaning it's not a good idea to tell support people what to do but, instead, to ask them to do something. They are happy to help but they don't want to be told what to do.

Take care of your people by helping them understand each other to support peak performance individually, as a team, and as a company.

If you want your business to grow, make sure you have really good systems in place first—before you start trying to grow too much—or you risk blowing up your team and your company. In our company, for example, we've grown 20 to 30% every year for nearly the last decade—that's manageable. We haven't doubled our growth every year because it's unmanageable; in fact, hardly anyone can keep up with that pace and do it well. Operations people like things to be steady vs. in constant chaos . . . and this is during the best mortgage market in history, where rates are in the twos and threes. Everybody's been so darn busy that you really have to make sure you're taking care of your people. Your systems can help reduce stress and growing pains for your team overall.

In every industry, sales and operations have opposing goals—delivering on a real-time deadline vs. covering the fine print with a project mindset. In our company, we focus on blending personalities and making sure people get along. There isn't a requirement to be best friends with everybody but it is important to get along as a team. Our goal is to help our clients have a great experience. We want them to have such a great experience that they refer us to other people. Our intention is to make the mortgage process a nice, solid, feel-good process because most of the time, unfortunately, it's not . . . the relationship makes the difference.

When our clients feel that relationship in action through our stellar service including our systems, professionalism, communications, and how we conduct business by putting the relationship first, the investment we make in relationships is obvious. In fact, that is the most significant investment you can make that predictably pays you back over time—help people get what they want. Generous people generate.

About Brett Lindquist

Brett Lindquist was destined to be in the mortgage business. His father was a hotel resident manager so Brett lived in hotels until he was 13 years old. When his parents bought their first house, Brett thought, "How do people do this?"

He went to college at Florida State University as a scholarship swimmer and captain of the swim team his senior year; he doubled-majored in finance and real estate. Upon his graduation, most of the mortgage loans were done by the big banks. Brett interviewed with a mortgage broker who got him interested in the business. That was when Brett started in the business in 1983 and he's been in it ever since.

In 1995, Brett co-founded The Mortgage Firm, a residential mortgage company that makes home ownership a reality. The company has experienced 15–20% growth for each of the past ten years. With 50 branches and over 600 employees, the company will close over $3.5 billion in loans in 2020.

Brett gives back to the community by serving on the board of governors of the business school and the Booster's at Florida State University. He is married to Cindy and has two fantastic children.

Brett can be reached at:

Email: **brett.lindquist@tmf.mortgage**

Phone: 321-277-3041

Website: **themortgagefirm.com/**

Design Your Life to Have It

By Roger McGuire, Jr.
Producing Branch Manager and Loan Originator
McGuire Lending Group powered by Success
Mortgage Partners

I became a loan officer for a number of reasons: 1) to use and parlay my degree in finance, 2) to have flexible work hours, and 3) to ensure my paycheck reflected my work ethic. I had worked in corporate America and—I say this with respect—discovered I am professionally unemployable in that environment (smile.) So I became a loan officer because I wanted my exceptionally strong work ethic to translate to a substantial paycheck as opposed to what I could earn in a traditional 40-hour work week. The opportunity to help homeowners fit my financial background and degree perfectly.

There were two significant challenges in my business that I had to resolve. The first being that, for quite some time after I opened my own branch, I was a one-man band with an amazing processor. It's exceedingly difficult to work ON the business when you're working IN the business. I was the proverbial butcher, baker, and candlestick maker. If we had an IT problem, I was the IT guy. When we had compliance issues, I was the compliance person. A lot of my workday was spent doing things I really didn't like doing—they didn't make me any money or contribute value to my customers.

My day was filled with things that kept my license on the wall and were important, but I had to do everything. I had an awesome processor and some help but trying to grow that one-man band was a big challenge.

The other significant challenge was that we moved to Florida and knew only one couple there at the time. Now, that one couple was a huge help to me. However, the truth is we had to grow a business with no database and no network—we had to grow it from zero. Moving to Florida was a decision that came out of a challenge I faced in my business in Chicago where I grew up.

A lot of people in Chicago hibernate in the winter real estate-wise, and rightfully so. When the weather is horrible with freezing temperatures and a foot of snow on the ground, nobody wants to go look at open houses on the weekend. It's not nearly as enticing as it is in the summer months. While we always had pretty solid winter seasons in business, it was a predictable struggle to figure out how to maintain business volume during those cold months when most people were not as active. In Florida, people are busy in Chicago's "off" season (winter) so we made the decision to move. That was a pivotal leap of faith that turned out well.

The Awesome List

To help overcome any challenge, it's important to work on yourself first. I chose to reach out to experienced people and get their guidance. I've had mentors and coaches since 2008, so finding that right coach was a big start toward achieving more of what I wanted. Second, a primary strategy was to have a great team whose expertise allowed me to get out of the file so our clients can have a better experience. That also allows me to do what I do with my strengths and talents to grow the business. Hiring a great team was huge for us. We have an amazing team right now. Third, I believe everything is about who you hang with so I joined a mastermind group with Carl White and Tammy Schneider. I joined the Freedom Club, which was a huge help for me because, no matter what I was trying to do in my career, there is always somebody in the Club who's done it already. To surround myself with like-minded people was a big help for both state of mind and practical resources.

In Florida, to overcome growth and development challenges, I did what we call the Awesome List. As I mentioned, I knew one couple when moving here. He is a great friend of mine and he is in real estate—he's fantastic. I said, "hey, you're awesome. Who else do you know who's awesome?" That's how we built our network. When we met anybody who we thought was a great fit for our Awesome List in terms of their quality, their business, and their character, we added them to our list. And then we asked them who else they knew just like them and we gravitated toward those people. Awesome people tend to hang out with awesome people or, as they say, eagles hang with eagles. So working on myself and then surrounding myself with awesome people both on my team and in the industry definitely inspired me to take my business to the next level.

The result of overcoming those challenges has been amazing. As with anything, success is not a straight line. Success can move like a heartbeat in some instances; the good news is, when you are on the right track, any momentary downward trends keep moving higher over time. My life is monumentally better after overcoming those challenges. In fact, resolving challenges has been the biggest factor in dramatically changing my business and my personal life. Obviously, I've closed a lot more loans. I think I've closed three times as many loans this year as I did the first year I met Carl back in 2016.

Personally, the results of doing the work has brought financial stability, which is a big, big relief. It doesn't matter what walk of life you're in—being financially unstable is exceedingly difficult and leads to a lot of stress. Asking for help and coming through the other side of those challenges brings financial stability which helps smooth a lot of things in life.

I say it is all about who you hang with and my family is paramount to everything I do. I am married to the greatest woman in the world—she is the main person who not only helped me get through these challenges, but lived them with me. These challenges were not just mine—they were ours as a couple and as a family. My hours when we moved to Florida—and this is no exaggeration—were that I would roll out of bed at 5:00 A.M. and, instead of going to the gym like I did in Chicago, I'd start working. My kids were two and four then. Since I was working out of the house, I'd come out to eat breakfast and lunch and I would finish my calls around 8:00 or 9:00 at night. That was every day, every week, and I worked a lot of weekends as well. Now, I'm out of work at a normal time and I almost never work weekends. I work late one night a week by design; other nights I'm done early enough to see all my kids' games—no more missed soccer, baseball, or lacrosse games. I've made it to every one of those games.

The better money and fewer hours is one outcome but, even more importantly, I'm a better dad and a better husband. I feel more accomplished with what I'm doing, like I'm making a bigger impact. When I'm working on details of a title or chasing docs or other things I'm not the greatest at, I don't feel like I'm making an impact. Now doing what I do using my natural strengths and preferences, I'm having a better impact, growing the team, and nurturing relationships with and for my referral sources as well as with my customers. My customer experience has always been good and now it has gotten even better. We deliver a fantastic customer experience because of the team we've built and the processes we put in place. The coolest part about it is that my wife and I are raising my kids where we want to retire. We didn't have to wait until we were retirement age to move to paradise—we're able to live that life well before retirement age. It's been really nice to have that kind of freedom as the reward for working so hard for it.

A Long Conversation

If I were to go back in time to ten years ago, I would have a long conversation with myself. The theme of that conversation would be to surround myself with the people I wanted to be like or who were already where I wanted to go professionally. In practical terms, that means finding the mastermind group specific to your field, like the Freedom Club has been for me. That's been just paramount to where I am today.

Ten years ago, I thought I was the only one in the mortgage world who cared deeply about clients and who also had a good work ethic and high character. When you join a group like the Freedom Club, you realize there are a lot of us out there who are very giving with their time, expertise, and advice. The cool part of participating in a group like that is you can also advise and share successes with other members. You are who you hang with . . . so choose wisely.

While a professional community is helpful, the adage of being who you hang out with is also about your everyday life which, for me, means team. You become a family in your business relationships, whether you like it or not. I've got a team of professionals in my business who are second to none. The people on my team are ridiculously fantastic at what they do, and they're even better people than they are great in their role.

Another thing I would tell myself is to prioritize family time and life balance. My oldest son was born ten years ago, which obviously changed my life. I've always been an incredibly involved and dedicated father, but you have to make a decision to carve out that time early on…which I did. I think I could, and want to, do more of it…so now I do. Carve out family time first and everything will fall into place. A wise man once told me if your life at home is great and work is not—life is still good. If your home life is not going well, it does not matter how great work is…life is pretty tough. Building work-life harmony should be your main priority and focus, then sort out your work. Work will find a way to fill in the space.

The only other thing I'd add is to find a platform and a system that works for you. I was on a broker platform ten years ago, which was great and I saw and did a lot of wonderful things. But the platform and model I'm in now is a substantially better fit than where I was ten years ago because I'm not doing everything on my own. I have help. Get help. Everybody needs good help.

Preach the Power is In Your People

The one strategy that has resulted in the most closed loans for me is maintaining the relationships with my clients and treating them like I want to be treated. We always tell our clients, "you're taking a mortgage for 30 years. Our relationship doesn't stop at the closing—that's when we really begin working together." We've done a fantastic job of staying in touch with our clients. Two thirds of my business is a combination of past clients coming back, past clients referring friends and family, or current clients introducing us to people they know, like, and trust.

Just as importantly, the relationships with my team are critical to our business success. The secret to building my team is that I truly 100% appreciate my team—and I let them know that as often as possible. One thing we do very well is maintain our client relationships. But I feel that's the third most important thing. The second most important thing is making sure our referral sources are happy. And the number one most important thing is my team's happiness.

My team has to be happy, energized, inspired, and feel empowered where we're at because when they feel that way, it will naturally roll into the referral source relationships, which rolls right into the client relationships. Employee happiness just results in a great experience for everyone. I preach having and keeping that family culture. We're incredibly open and authentic. We collaborate. We share game plans, ideas, goals, the process...and then I just get out of their way.

My wife and I have a phrase: 'helping is not always helping.' For example, when she is working on a project and I jump in to help, she gives me that look—the one that says I can best help by getting out of the way. It's a tongue in cheek joke, but I've taken that phrase and applied it to the work environment too. When you have a great team, just let them do their thing. Trying to help sometimes means not helping so I just let them do what they know to do. In fact, they tell me what to do. We go over the process, the game plan, and the end game but my team is definitely empowered. I appreciate them. The business culture we have created together is fantastic.

Working with a coach and a mentor has helped me tremendously. In 2008 when the market crashed, I found my first coaching group, which had a lot of various business professionals—they were a great help. When I moved to Florida, I needed that same kind of support that I left behind in Illinois, but more industry-specific. That's when I joined Carl's group. The fact we are in the same field, with him being an active branch manager, helped a lot. For me, having a coach and mentor is an absolute necessity. They're a good accountability partner. You're not reinventing the wheel while becoming more successful. You find people who've "been there / done that" level of success in life and business so they clarify what that exactly means and then they teach you how to reach it.

If I had to come up with a Mount Rushmore of the people in my life who have impacted it positively and who are not named mom, dad, wife, or brother, Carl is on that Mount Rushmore. He's absolutely been a huge part of where I'm at and where I'm going. His ability to listen, coach, and give advice are unparalleled, and his expertise is off the charts. I have the ability to over-complicate things sometimes. I put too many things on my plate and Carl's superpower is to simplify it. He says, "The main thing is to keep the main thing the main thing." It's profound and helpful in its straightforward clarity. If you don't have a coach, you absolutely 100% need one as a necessity to being successful.

Surround with Inspiration

If I could offer advice to other loan officers, the number one thing is to decide what you love to do, what you're good at, and what makes you money (we call that the Triad of Awesomeness in The Freedom Club)—then just do that and delegate the rest. That's really the key to success. When you can find and delegate the rest of what's needed to create success to people who love those aspects of the job, and they're really good at them, it makes the company money. It makes you happier. You're helping other people have a livelihood. So that's the main thing—decide what you love to do and what you're good at, then go do it and make some money so you can delegate the rest.

I would also recommend surrounding yourself only with people who inspire you and make you better, and who you can likewise inspire. My wife and I preach this concept to our kids too. You are who you hang with and that is a decision. Where you can, strategically surround yourself with people who make you better and hold you accountable to the standard of where you should be and where you're going to help you get there.

Something that has worked out very well for me is taking the mortgage profession and making it a virtual one. I get to live in paradise and do loans everywhere. There could be a snowstorm in Chicago and I'm in shorts and a t-shirt in Florida helping people out. That remote work model has worked out really well for both my lifestyle and for growing the business. It's been huge, actually. Plugging into the banker model, with Success Mortgage Partners, has been a huge part of being successful too because it allows me to focus on the things I love to do, the things I'm good at and the things that make me money.

I'm really happy with where my life is today. I'm in a really good sweet spot. Within two years, I will double my business and I will do that within the work-life balance parameters I've worked so hard to achieve. That's really my focus as far as business is concerned: doubling our business without it being at the expense of my peace of mind and time with my wife and kids, and the same thing for my team. We don't want anyone on our team working 15 hour days either. The way to get there at this point is for me to continue getting out of the way for my team and focusing on my main activities.

I've got a great team that we invested a lot of time building. I'm literally just now at the point where we have the capacity to double my business yet again. I have a team who can do it. At this point, I finally have the freedom to just focus on the main things I do that bring in more business for us. It will allow us to, at the very least, double our business in the next two years while still allowing me to spend time with my favorite people on earth—my wife and kiddos.

Prove What Is Possible

You can do anything you want. You have to have a plan and stick to it. When I moved to Florida, there were a lot of people who told me I couldn't do it. They said my business and home life would falter and I would be just another lender in Florida. I didn't listen to those people. I listened to my coaches and mentors. I found more help in that arena and chose to listen and follow the people who said I could do it. And I did...I proved to everyone what's possible.

So whatever life you want to design, it is absolutely 100% obtainable. Just come up with a game plan and the consistent behaviors you need to make it happen. When you take the right steps in the right order, the only possible outcome will be your success. It's just a matter of time and execution to make it happen.

Take it from me . . . you can live wherever you want, that's for darn sure. No more blizzards. No more snow. No more shoveling. So what life do you really want?

About Roger McGuire, Jr.

I am married to the greatest woman on earth and father of the two coolest boys ever. My favorite thing to do is to spend quality time with my family—whether it is enjoying living in paradise or traveling in our RV, we love to find new adventures and experiences to do together.

I began my mortgage career in 2001 and opened my own branch in 2005. The foundation of my business is our Client Service Program, where the relationship with our clients begins at the closing instead of ending at the closing. We consistently manage our clients' mortgages and introduce those clients to trusted advisers that can assist them in both maintaining their homes and their livelihoods well into the future.

Specialties: We specialize in the following services for our valued customers.

- Owner Occupied, Second Homes and Investment Properties for Purchase or Refinance
- Reverse Mortgages
- First Time Home Buyers
- FHA Loans

Roger can be reached at:

Email: **team@mcguirelending.com**

Phone: Illinois office (630) 971-1901 or
Florida office (941) 212-2665

Website: **mcguirelending.com**

Facebook: **facebook.com/mcguirelending/**

LinkedIn: **linkedin.com/in/roger-mcguire-jr-46b3298/**

Going for the Triple Double

By Hakim Singleton
Branch Manager
Singleton Mortgage

I'm a city kid, born and raised. I'm from North Philadelphia and, while some people called it 'the hood,' I called it home. I fell into the mortgage business by accident. In college, I took an internship with a rural farm lending company. I had to drive an hour and a half each way for my new job—it was the first time I had ever been out of the city for anything other than fun.

To say it was an eye-opening experience doesn't do it justice. Here I was...a young black man from the city working with a primarily Amish community whose members barely drove cars and knew little about technology. It was my first lesson in diversity. And it was an amazing experience with an amazing group of people that taught me a lot about life, humanity, and myself. It was my job to find people who needed to purchase farm equipment or build additions on their farms and then help them refinance their renovations.

I've often been asked why I would drive an hour and a half one-way to a place I'd never been to service people who weren't like me. All I can say is I knew I wanted more for myself. I didn't want to be a product of my surroundings or my neighborhood. I was determined to be successful so I took that leap.

At the time, I drove a 1999 Chrysler. That car broke down more times than it got me to where I was going. However, in that experience, I learned the impact affordable financing can make on a family. When your housing costs are lowered, you can afford better things—like a car that actually worked.

One internship led to another, the next being with a large bank. It was then I decided to pursue a mortgage career. As soon as that internship ended, I got my first job and found my first loan—a reverse mortgage. Nothing like jumping in with both feet, right?

I will never forget that experience or the woman I met for that deal. Her story made a big impact on my life. She called our hotline one day, and I was lucky enough to answer the phone. She explained her situation to me and it hit my heart. She was an elderly lady living off a fixed income of $700 a month from Social Security; however, her mortgage was $740 a month. Her children tried to help as best as they could but they were struggling as well. She received food stamps but they didn't tide her through the end of the month.

I worked hard to get her that mortgage. By the time we were through, she no longer was paying a mortgage but instead was getting paid $200 a month! I realized then and there the impact I could make in someone's life—and I've never looked back.

With my first mortgage under my belt, I thought I was on my way. However, I struggled trying to drum up business. My manager, an amazing guy who is still in the business, sat me down and said "Hakim, you have to be willing to go where other people are not willing to go. You have to be willing to do what other lenders aren't willing to do because their pockets are fat. They're happy right now." He told me he had cut his teeth doing loans in west Philadelphia and in southwest Philadelphia in the Navy Yard because he had connections there. He suggested I go to where I had connections. So I started going to where I knew—the hood in North Philly.

The Magic of Pretzels

I hit the pavement and literally walked on foot, knocking on real estate office doors and delivering cupcakes, cookies, and pretzels to bribe my way past the gatekeepers. Back then, I didn't have the help of social media so I had to do things the old-school way—driving around town and knocking on doors.

I met with a local business owner who made pretzels and convinced them to sell them to me at a discount. Through persistence, perseverance, and consistency, I saw business start to come my way. My clients were all trying to make a better life for themselves. They were looking to improve the dynamics for their family, to just live in a safe neighborhood, and have better schools for their kids. It drove me to work harder to help them find a better life.

I began to grow a reputation for getting tough loans done. From that day until now, my loan practice has been primarily focused on tough loans and helping people get out of bad situations. It's been an amazing ride.

I'll admit this past year was tough for me. With the refi boom, rate compression, and Covid, my business went from a full pipeline to an empty one—overnight. I decided then and there I needed to diversify my portfolio so that wouldn't happen again. I've spent the last year reinventing and rebuilding my business. I still want to help people in tough situations, but I also want to grow my business and get to the next level.

The growing pains have been real. I've been developing my systems and processes, hiring and training a team, and finding new sources for referrals. Some people might call it a grind, but I call it growing a business and creating a legacy for my family.

Be Willing to Do What Others Won't

I have a wife and three small children. It has not been easy to juggle work and family. Growing a business from scratch is hard. When I worked for the bank, we focused primarily on refinances. However, I realized quickly that was not a sustainable model so I've had to work at growing my purchase business. For me, it's been a lot of long hours courting realtor relationships and networking in my community. There have been times my wife felt she was raising our kids alone. We've had to stay in constant communication to keep our marriage strong.

I love football. And I love analogies. So I compare what I am going through to what a quarterback must go through to be great. Just like Tom Brady has had to study plays, get up early to work out, lead a team, and then encourage that team, I find I have to do the same in my mortgage business. I have to know my craft, I have to lead my team, I have to encourage that team, and I have to get up early to go find my business.

I've become disciplined. I have activities I must do every single day to grow my company. And I am translating that focus into being disciplined at home as well. I am making time to court my wife, help raise our children, and to be a better man. It's tough trying to run a business, grow that business, and maintain my family. But I know when I cook breakfast for my wife even when I'm tired, it's making a positive deposit into her emotional bank account. The bigger her emotional bank account, the better our relationship. So I do the hard things especially when it would be easier not to do them.

As my early career mentor told me, "You have to do the things no one else is willing to do." I've also heard "live today like no one else so you can live tomorrow like no one else." Those sayings remind me why I'm working hard at my business and at home—so I can give myself and my family the future we want.

The Triple Double

In basketball, there is something called the triple double. It consists of 10 rebounds, 10 assists, and 10 points. I'm shooting for the triple double in my life! I want to be a 10 as a father, a 10 in my marriage as a husband, and a 10 at work as a leader and loan officer. When I'm a great dad, my kids do well. When I'm a great husband, my wife does well. And when I'm a great entrepreneur and employer, my employees do well and I bring in money—and everybody wins. I want to have it all—and I know I can so I'm willing to do what I need to do to make it happen.

I don't want just financial freedom. I'm also looking for freedom in my time and freedom from stress. What does it profit a man to have all the money in the world if he comes home to a sad house? Money may turn the electricity and the heat on but it doesn't keep you warm at night or your heart warm.

The One Thing

If I could go back in time and have a talk with my younger self, I would say to remember that it's not all about the money. I would tell myself to be patient, save money, never stop believing in myself, and to trust God. I would say don't quit, stay focused, and don't get sidetracked. And, finally, I would tell myself to forgive the people who hurt me in my past.

I believe in building relationships. That's how I grow my business. I think the one thing that has served me best is reaching out to real estate agents and seeing if they're a good match for doing business like I do. The easiest way to meet an agent is if they are the listing agent on one of my purchases. I'll give them a call and invite them to meet for coffee. If I'm not meeting enough agents that way, I will attend realtor association meetings.

In fact, I met one of my favorite brokers at one of those kinds of meetings. I was sitting at a table and a broker walked over and smiled and said "I just had to come to meet you, your smile is infectious. You have a great spirit!" I said "You too!!!" The following week, I met her at her office about an hour away in Limerick, Pennsylvania. I continued to drive to her office and meet with her every single week for three years. Recently, she said "Hakim, I want to partner with you and have you come into our office here and be our lender." That day, all the way home, I cried—literally cried. I worked so hard for this and it had finally paid off.

That one "chance" meeting turned out to be the best thing that ever happened in my career. It led to many other opportunities and many other meetings with agents outside of Philadelphia. Their buyers are highly qualified. The sales prices are higher, the credit scores are better, and the loans are much easier to write. Those three years of grit changed my life. Those 158 weeks of "no, not yet" taught me perseverance and determination and, in the end, helped me get to where I am today.

If I had to pick a second "something" that has really helped me get to the next level, it's building my team. I had a junior loan officer who worked for me several years ago; she did not like to go out and drum up business. My gut told me to give her a call and see if she wanted to come to work for me again as my loan partner. Although she didn't want to sell, she bought into my vision and believed in me when others didn't. We make a great team! I go out and get the business and she helps me get it closed. She keeps me out of the weeds so I have time to go and sell. That kind of teamwork is invaluable.

Stay In the Draft

My good friend, mentor and coach, Carl White, always says, "stay in the draft." A draft is when two or more vehicles group together so closely that it reduces the drag on both cars so they both go much faster than they could on their own. Carl encourages us to surround ourselves with people who have the same dreams, goals, and drive as we do. Share with those people, dream with them, and then together make your business better.

As an athlete, I've had many coaches. Some told me what to do and some just gave me perspective and let me choose what to do. Whichever method, they have all helped me be a better version of myself. Coaching has taught me to shift my mindset from avoiding the "no" to accepting it and always looking for a "yes."

Another great thing Carl always says is, "you want a yes or a no—there is no money in maybes." I have found that "no" doesn't hurt as bad as I thought it did at the beginning. I realize now I have to get several no's to get a yes—and I'm OK with that now.

Through coaching, I've gained confidence. I KNOW I can make it rain! That has boosted my confidence in a big way. Through the turmoil of last year, guidelines changed and people lost their jobs. Like some loan officers, I lost most of my pipeline, which was scary. A quick call to my coach helped settle my mind and re-focus my energies on what I could do instead of what I couldn't do.

One night, I ordered pizza for my kids and, as I placed my order, a thought came into my mind. "How many of my referral partners are struggling right now because of the change in the market? Maybe I could do something nice for them and buy dinner for them and their families." Instantly, I felt gratitude for all that I had in my life. I decided to order pizzas for some of my real estate partners. I figured I had to eat, and my partners had to eat, so why not share a meal together. My intention was for us to laugh, chat, and share a meal together virtually. One thing led to another and the Virtual Pizza Party was born.

I invited 25 agents to my first "party." My local Domino's pizza place had touch-free delivery. I invited the top agents I already knew and worked with as well as a few agents I wasn't working with yet who were on my target list. I asked what kind of pizza they wanted and had it delivered to their homes. The first thirty minutes of that Zoom call were when our families shared dinner together. Afterwards, the professionals stayed on and shared what was working for business, what struggles we were having, and what we could do to help each other. That small idea became a main driver for my business.

It wasn't about the pizza. It was about reaching out to my fellow man, caring enough to ask how they were, and just seeing how I could help them. Most were surprised at first but thankful I had thought of them. I didn't ask for business in those meetings but my phone started ringing.

In that first party alone, I picked up two real estate agents who are now regular referral partners, closed seven transactions, and have 16 more pre-approved buyers looking for homes. One of my agents mentioned her daughter wanted to get into the business. Another agent volunteered to help her. One agent was unhappy where they were and connected with another agent and changed companies. Both are extremely happy now.

We have had several parties since then and I plan on making

them a regular part of my business. But, like other experiences in life, you never forget your first.

Double Down

When the tough times come, it shows you what you're made of. When I lost my pipeline, I could have sat around being depressed. Believe me, there were some moments when I was tempted to do that. Instead, like earlier in my career, I decided I needed to double down. Instead of calling 30 agents, I called 60. Instead of calling two or three people a day from my past database, I called four to six. Instead of calling my people under contract once a week, I called them twice a week and asked them for a referral. I learned to take a lemon and make lemonade.

During that time, I found it much easier to reach people since everyone was staying at home—a still target is much easier to hit than a moving one. The result was pretty amazing. In a very short time, I had rebuilt my pipeline with more qualified clients.

Be Nice

I don't want to brag so I will tell you what others say about me. Most say I am the nicest, most genuine, helpful, hard-working person they know. Being genuine and authentic has probably helped me the most in my business. I treat everyone equally, and instead of having a chip on my shoulder because of where I came from, I use it to motivate me to be a better person and to help others.

I have found that authenticity does not come back to a void; instead, it attracts other authentic people and makes for better and more tangible relationships. I won't go out and try and be someone I am not—I am Hakim.

The Ripple Effect

The future is bright for my business. I plan on continuing to grow my team and to recruit loan officers underneath me and help them grow their businesses. I see my current staff moving into positions of leadership. I see myself changing the lives of hundreds more people. Sometimes when I stop and think about it, I remember all the people I've already helped who have, in turn, been able to help others. It is a ripple effect. I know when I help a family, I'm also helping their extended family.

For example, I helped a family move out of the city and into a nicer suburban area. The schools are better and they feel safer. Their family has been visiting them and now have been inspired to make the move as well. I love knowing that I have had a positive effect on hundreds of people personally, but also maybe thousands I am unaware of and will never meet.

My final words of advice are to chase your dreams. Get after it—know you can be and do better. If I can do it, you can too. Also, know that if you don't stand and believe in yourself, you'll fall for anything. So stand for yourself and what you believe in, then go after your dreams and goals. Remember this is a marathon, not a sprint—success doesn't happen overnight.

In closing, I'd like to quote Nipsey Hussite, a rap artist who was tragically murdered in 2019. He said, "Before you run your race, you gotta find a pace, just make sure you cross the line and forget how long it takes." (That's the clean version.) We ARE in a marathon and my race is going to look different than your race. Don't compare yourself to others; instead, compare yourself to who you were yesterday and try to be a better version of yourself everyday. Live large and encourage others. Now go get it!

About Hakim Singleton

Hakim Singleton, Leader of Singleton Mortgage Group Powered by Success Mortgage Partners NMLS id 440468 in Phoenixville, Pennsylvania, has over 12 years of experience in both the retail banking and mortgage industries. As a licensed mortgage originator, Hakim is dedicated to helping clients achieve the dream of homeownership while keeping all stakeholders informed throughout the mortgage process.

He became a loan officer through an internship with a rural farm lending company. Having grown up in 'the hood,' this job was the first time he'd been out of the city. He worked with the Amish community and met some amazing people. When that internship ended, he took another one with a big bank, which is when he decided to pursue mortgage loan banking as a career.

Hakim believes the most important thing in business is the development of strong relationships. He is known for working very closely with first-time buyers, move-up buyers, and empty-nesters. No matter the situation, he and his team treats clients like family and tailors their services to support their unique needs. There is nothing more rewarding than seeing clients at the closing table— that goal motivates the entire mortgage process.

Today, Hakim is married with children, happily giving generously to his family and community, relentlessly going for his Triple Double.

Hakim can be reached at:

Email: **hakim@singletonmortgage.com**

Phone: 610-881-6496

Website: **singletonmortgage.com** | **HakimSingleton.com**

Instagram: **itsdakeemshow**

Summary and Next Action Steps

Over the course of my career, I've learned a lot—some of those lessons were painful. I've seen a lot too ... loan officers with tremendous heart who struggle, and loan officers who figured out their success formula by trying everything that didn't work first. The good news is you have the power in you to uplevel your business, regardless of your current level of success, when you start working smarter instead of harder.

I learned that lesson at my family's kitchen table from Uncle Dave when he told me to find and then sit next to the prettiest girl in my new college class and borrow her notes. He said if I did that, I would get what I needed to pass that class. Not only did I pass that class, I found my soulmate who is now my wife, Maria. A little strategy can go a long way in changing your life and business.

Through what you read in these pages, you can see that grit, strategy, heart, and taming challenges large and small are what forge loan officer champions. It's been my privilege to work with each and every one of them. The stories here are from real people just like you. Ideally, you now feel inspired and reassured that you are a loan officer champion in the making too. And I'd love to hear your stories as you go.

What challenges are you facing? What's working for you? And what do you wish was working for you? Let me know what challenges you're currently tackling because you're not in this alone. My team and I have your back. So fill me in, even if all you have is a renewed commitment to doing something different—I want to support you in that.

Take a few minutes to check out the resources at the back of this book...schedule your bonus gift strategy session to see the opportunities you have to change things up in your business, then visit our Facebook page at **Facebook.com/LoanOfficerBreakfastClub/** to share your takeaways from what you read in these powerhouse case studies.

I look forward to hearing your stories and celebrating your wins.

—Carl

The Freedom Club

The Most Powerful Group of Loan Officers in the World to Help You Get Better Clients, Close More Deals, Enhance Your Income

If you're a loan officer or Branch Manager closing six loans a month or more, then The Freedom Club is for you. As a member, you'll receive all the awesome benefits of Mortgage Marketing Animals.

In addition, you will have access to our full library of scripts for every occasion; loan checklists, systems and processes; job descriptions and ads; tracking sheets for leads, prospects, closings, and conversion rates; employee manuals; advanced loan-getting strategies and more.

Mastermind retreats every 90–120 days with other top-producing members are also included. Most importantly, you will receive personalized, one-on-one accountability coaching every two weeks. Here a plan will be designed specifically around you, your team, your market and your goals for the future.

Want a sneak peek at what it means to be in The Freedom Club? Check it out here:

FreedomClubApplication.com

If you have any questions, just give us a call at **(727) 787-2275.**

Be A Guest on the Podcast

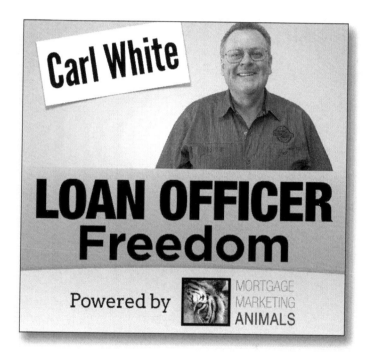

In a weekly podcast, Carl brings you the best and brightest in personal interviews to discover the keys to success that are working in the field. This podcast is dedicated to inspiring loan officers to take the best of what they know to help them create the business results and lifestyle they really want.

Carl's style is casual, down-to-earth and practical. He empowers listeners while entertaining them and sharing tools, stories and strategies that can accelerate their mortgage loan business results. Check out the podcast here:

LoanOfficerFreedom.com/

And if you would like to be considered for a guest spot on the show, just call our office at **(727) 787-2275**—we'd love to share your success strategies!

About Carl White

I am a husband, and a father to three wonderful young adults. My family and I enjoy boating, camping, and I am passionate about traveling the country on my Harley Davidson while masterminding with the top thought leaders in the world.

On the business side of things, I am the Founder/ Chief Strategist of The Mortgage Marketing Animals and also the host of the #1 Podcast for loan officers in America.

I first began my venture into the mortgage business as a loan officer in October of 1999. Within eight months of opening the doors at Family First Mortgage, I became the top-producing branch out of approximately 336 branches nationwide. I also began to train fellow loan officers in my "paint by numbers" approach. This technique helped the LO's retain more closings while working less hours in a week. Five years later, I opened my own mortgage business called Time Mortgage.

Who I Help:

I help loan officers to implement proven marketing strategies I have personally used in my own career and had great success with, measured by hundreds of thousands of dollars in revenue each and every month. While I make no income claims for you (of course), it is my belief I may be able to help you increase yours.

How I Help:

I show specific step-by-step instructions on how to drastically increase your monthly loan production and income while working only 32 hours per week. I do this by teaching loan officers to hyper-focus their efforts, and to stop doing wasteful activities they are currently doing that are not producing measurable results. By following the strategies I provide, my clients are able to regain the freedom to do the things they want to do. Worrying about when and where the next deal will come from is no longer a concern.

Specialties:

Strategizing | Marketing | Advising | Speaking
Video Blogging | Marketing Seminars | Marketing Webinars
Generating Leads | Social Media Marketing | Video Marketing

Carl can be reached at:

Email: **carl.white@TheMarketingAnimals.com**

Phone: 727-787-2275

Website: **MortgageMarketingAnimals.com/**

Facebook: **Facebook.com/MortgageMarketingAnimals**

LinkedIn: **LinkedIn.com/in/MarketingAnimals**

Podcast: **LoanOfficerFreedom.com/**

Instagram: **@themarketinganimals**

Made in the USA
Columbia, SC
29 October 2022